Fundamentals
of Our Faith

HERSCHEL H. HOBBS

BROADMAN
&HOLMAN
PUBLISHERS

Nashville, Tennessee

© 1960 • Broadman Press
Nashville, Tennessee
All rights reserved
International copyright secured

ISBN: 0-8054-1702-8
4217-02

Library of Congress catalog card number 60-5200

Printed in the United States of America

To

the members of the

FIRST BAPTIST CHURCH

Oklahoma City, Oklahoma

whose continuance through the years
"in the apostles' doctrine and fellowship" has made our ministry with
them truly a labor of love.

Introduction

THIS VOLUME BEGAN as a series of prayer meeting messages growing out of the conviction that Baptist people should "be ready always to give an answer to every man that asketh you a reason of the hope that is in you" (1 Peter 3:15). While there are many books dealing with Baptist doctrines, none served within itself to treat the matter in exactly the manner that we had in mind. For that reason we prepared in outline form, with discussion, the topics selected for study and distributed mimeographed copies to those present at a given prayer service. At the outset the outlines were not prepared with any idea of publication. However, so great was the response and so numerous the requests from our members and from other pastors for additional copies that we came to feel that there might be value in a wider distribution.

Admittedly the material in these studies is a mixture of my own ideas and those borrowed from others. I have sought to give credit for that portion found in other published works. At times I have followed rather closely the outline and content of E. Y. Mullins' *The Christian Religion in Its Doctrinal Expression,* a standard work in systematic theology.

The use made of this volume and others was in the hope that some of the most profound truths which make up our Baptist faith might be presented in simple and concise form. Of course, not all facets of that belief have been included, but the limits of space prohibit such a treatment.

This work is not intended to be understood as an official statement of Baptist belief. It is simply the effort of one Baptist to set forth his own understanding of that body of beliefs commonly held by Baptists.

Throughout this study copious Scripture references have been cited for the benefit of those desiring to make a more thorough study of these doctrines. Transliterations of certain key Hebrew and Greek words are included simply to familiarize the average reader with their distinctions. Unless otherwise indicated, all references are taken from the King James Version of the Bible. It is to be hoped that many will be as noble as the people of Berea, who "searched the scriptures daily, whether those things were so" (Acts 17:11).

The use of footnotes has been avoided in order to conserve space. Instead, parenthetical references for quoted material, general ideas followed without quotation, and references to other works suggested for further study have been given. These various references will include the following works:

BROADUS, JOHN A. *Commentary on the Gospel of Matthew* ("An American Commentary on the New Testament Series," ed. Alvah Hovey, Vol. I). Philadelphia: American Baptist Publication Society, 1886.

CARVER, W. O. *The Glory of God in the Christian Calling.* Nashville: Broadman Press, 1949.

FAIRBAIRN, A. M. *The Philosophy of the Christian Religion.* New York: George H. Doran Co., 1902.

HOBBS, HERSCHEL H. *Studies in Hebrews*. Nashville: Broadman Press, 1954.

———. *Who Is This?* Nashville: Broadman Press, 1952.

HODGES, J. W. *Christ's Kingdom and Coming*. Grand Rapids: Wm. B. Eerdmans Publishing Co., 1957.

LINDSAY, THOMAS M. *The Church and the Ministry in the Early Centuries*. London: Hodder & Stoughton, 1902.

MARSTON, CHARLES. *The Bible Comes Alive*. London: Eyre and Spottiswood, 1940.

MULLINS, EDGAR YOUNG. *The Christian Religion in Its Doctrinal Expression*. Nashville: Sunday School Board of the Southern Baptist Convention, 1917.

RAMM, BERNARD. *The Christian View of Science and Scripture*. Grand Rapids: Wm. B. Eerdmans Publishing Co., 1954.

ROBERTSON, A. T. *Studies in the Text of the New Testament*. Nashville: Sunday School Board of the Southern Baptist Convention, 1926.

SMITH, WILBUR M. *Therefore, Stand*. Boston: W. A. Wilde Company, 1945.

STEVENSON, HERBERT F. *Titles of the Triune God*. Westwood, N. J.: Fleming H. Revell Company, 1956.

The International Standard Bible Encyclopaedia, ed. James Orr. Chicago: The Honard Severance Company, 1915.

THAYER, JOSEPH H. *A Greek-English Lexicon of the New Testament*. New York: The American Book Company, 1889.

TURNER, CLYDE J. *These Things We Believe*. Nashville: Convention Press, 1956.

I am indebted to many people for many things which have made this presentation possible: to my family, who have been denied many hours of fellowship; to Stanton H. Nash, my valued associate, from whom came the original suggestion for this series; to Lucile Gibson, my secretary, who has worked beyond the call of duty; to many members of my church, who first heard these studies given; to many publishers, who have granted permission to glean ideas from their publications; but, most of all, "to him that is of power to stablish you according to my gospel, and the preaching of Jesus Christ, according to the revelation of the mystery, which was kept secret since the world began, but now is made manifest, and by the scriptures of the prophets, according to the commandment of the everlasting God, made known to all nations for the obedience of faith: to God only wise, be glory through Jesus Christ for ever. Amen" (Rom. 16:25–27) .

Contents

1

The Bible

> *The grass withereth, and the flower thereof falleth away: but the word of the Lord endureth for ever. And this is the word by which the gospel is preached unto you.*   1 PETER 1:24–25

THE WORD "BIBLE" is a transliteration of the Greek word *biblos*, which referred to the inner bark of the papyrus plant (note the English word "paper") and meant "book." The Bible is God's divine library containing sixty-six books, thirty-nine in the Old Testament and twenty-seven in the New Testament. The Old Testament was originally written in Hebrew, the New Testament in Greek. While there are many translations, the final voice as to meaning is the original language itself in the light of the historical environment involved. The Bible is the source book of the Christian's faith.

If the Bible is discarded, Christians are like a ship without rudder or compass. Believers need a source of authority in religion. The Roman Catholic relies upon the authority of the Church, which finds its sources of truth in tradition and the Scriptures. By their own admission, to Catholics tradition is of the greater importance. Baptists find their source of authority in the Bible alone. Where it speaks, they speak. Where it is silent, they are silent. While not rejecting other sources of knowledge, Baptists insist that they must neither deny nor displace the Bible. No proven knowledge has done so.

I. The Bible Is an Inspired Book

Three words are necessary in discussing this great truth. Revelation is the process by which God unveils himself and his will to human messengers (Gen. 12:1; Ex. 20:1; Isa. 6:1–8; Jer. 1:2; Rev. 1:1). Illumination is the spiritual understanding imparted by God's Holy Spirit to enable man to grasp the truth revealed (John 14:16–17, 25–26). Inspiration is the inbreathing of the Holy Spirit whereby the human messenger is divinely guided in delivering or recording God's message (Jer. 1:9; Ezek. 1:3; Gal. 1:11–12). This does not mean that the writer made no effort to secure the facts about which he wrote. In the preface of his Gospel Luke said, "It seemed good to me also, having traced all things accurately from the first, to write" (1:3, author's translation).

There are two schools of thought as to the method of inspiration. The verbal inspiration group insists that God inspired every word and that the writer was merely a stenographer. The thought inspiration school holds that God inspired the ideas but that the writer expressed them in his own words. By whatever method used, the Holy Spirit guarded the authors from error as they wrote what God wanted them to say.

1. Inspiration.—The Bible claims inspiration. While not the final voice in such a consideration, the internal evidence of its claim to inspiration must be heard. "For the prophecy came not in old time by the will of man: but holy men of God spake as they were moved by [picked up and borne along by] the Holy Ghost" (2 Peter 1:21). "And Moses wrote all the words of the Lord" (Ex. 24:4).

The prophets spoke by inspiration. "Hear, O heavens, and give ear, O earth: for the Lord hath spoken" (Isa. 1:2). "Thus speaketh the Lord God of Israel, saying, Write thee all the words that I have spoken unto thee in a book" (Jer. 30:2). Jesus said, "But the Comforter, which is the Holy Ghost [Spirit], . . . he shall teach you all things, and bring all things to your remembrance, whatsoever I have said unto you" (John 14:26). "Howbeit when he, the Spirit of truth, is come, he will guide you into all truth: . . . and he will shew you things to come" (John 16:13). Paul concluded, "All scripture is given by inspiration of God [God-breathed]" (2 Tim. 3:16).

2. *Unity.*—The Bible is a unit. The Bible was written by approximately fifty-seven different authors from all walks of life—farmers, shepherds, tentmakers, physicians, governors, and kings. The span of its writing was about fifteen hundred years in places ranging all the way from Babylon to Rome. It deals with history, law, poetry, prophecy, philosophy, science, sociology, and salvation, to mention only a few of its varied themes.

The Bible was not written by its authors with the purpose of forming one book. Yet, gathered together under the guidance of the Holy Spirit in its final form after A.D. 300, it tells one complete story. If one should read the New Testament without a knowledge of the Old Testament, he would ask, "Where is that which went before?" If he should read the Old Testament without knowing the New Testament, he would inquire, "Where is the rest of the story?" The only reasonable answer is that all this was done under the guiding hand of God.

3. Divinity.—The Bible is divine in its contents. In comparison with literature contemporary with it the Bible excels all else. One has but to read the books of the Apocrypha to verify this. A comparison with the pseudo-gospels of the first two centuries after Christ places the four canonical Gospels above them as the heavens are above the earth.

The Bible contains truth not to be found in any other book. While man may discover some truth about God through nature and reason, as the Greek philosophers did, it is quite evident that the message of the Bible far exceeds such sources of knowledge. The truth of the Bible was not discovered by "natural man" but was revealed to men by the Holy Spirit (1 Cor. 2:14). Nor can we exhaust the meaning of the Bible. It is timely and timeless as to its teachings. A person can learn all there is to know about other literature, but not about the Bible. This can be said of no other book.

The Bible comprises a complete whole. It is not only a record of prophecy but the fulfilment thereof. Our Lord himself found in its contents the message of God. From no other book did he quote, but its citations were often on his lips (Matt. 4:7; 12:40; 21:42; Luke 24:27).

4. Survival.—The Bible is unique in its survival. If any other book had been subjected to the destructive efforts aimed at the Bible, it would long since have disappeared. Through fire and flood the Bible has come down through the centuries, floating upon a river of martyrs' blood.

Although some seek today to label the Bible as a "Catholic book," the record of history is to the contrary. While it is true that until the invention of the printing press (A.D. 1454) Bible manuscripts were copied by monks, it is also true that the Catholic governments of Europe did all they could do to destroy it. Other European governments controlled by state churches followed their lead in suppressing the Bible. Stories excelling best-seller thrillers relate the struggle to place the Bible in the hands of the common people.

For centuries the Bible, written only in Latin, was a closed book to all but the educated clergy and intelligentsia outside the clergy. A small group of men labored to wrest it from these and place it in the hands of the ordinary man. We relate two incidents. (For a fuller treatment see Robertson, *Studies in the Text of the New Testament.*)

John Wycliffe's contribution, the first translation from the Latin into the people's tongue, was done in the face of stiff opposition from the constituted religious and civil authorities. So popular was his work that men would pay a load of hay for the privilege of reading it for one hour. After Wycliffe's death he was denounced by the Archbishop of Canterbury as "that pestilent wretch of damnable memory, son of the old sea serpent, yea the forerunner and disciple of the antichrist, who as the complement of his wickedness, invented a new translation of the Scriptures into his mother tongue." One monk called Wycliffe "the organ of the devil, the enemy of the Church, the idol of heretics, the image of hypocrites, the restorer of schism, the storehouse of lies, the sink of flattery." In 1415 the Council of Constance condemned his writings and his bones to the flames.

Perhaps the most thrilling story is that of William Tyndale, who printed the first Bible in English. With the coming of the Renaissance "Greece rose from the grave with the New Testament in her hand." This, together with the invention of the printing press, stimulated a new interest in the translation and distribution of the Scriptures. In 1516 Erasmus published his Greek New Testament. His dream was "for the day when the husbandman shall sing to himself portions of the Scriptures as he follows the plough, when the weaver shall hum them to the tune of his shuttle, when the traveler shall while away with their stories the weariness of his journey." This longing took root in the soul of William Tyndale, a student of Erasmus.

Putting his longing into action, Tyndale began translating the Scriptures from Greek into English. In 1524, in the face of stiff opposition, he fled to Germany where, under the protection of Martin Luther, he continued his work. Even there he encountered opposition. From Cologne he fled to Worms. There he completed and printed the first translation into English of the Greek New Testament ever made.

It is said that he finished setting his type late one afternoon. During the night vandals destroyed the type. But patiently he resumed the task, finishing it by the end of 1525. The next year he smuggled Bibles into England in sacks of flour. They were joyfully received by the people, but the bishops sent agents to buy and destroy them. However, the Bibles continued to come until the country was flooded with copies of the New Testament in English. As the result of this work Tyndale was arrested and on October 6, 1536, was strangled and burned. His dying prayer was, "Lord, open the King of England's eyes." His prayer was answered with the publication of the King James Version of the Bible in 1611.

Surely no one can read such accounts without seeing the hand of God in it all. Even with the authoritative Church and state opposed to it, the Bible came through to victory. Surely the same Holy Spirit who inspired the Bible also worked to preserve it!

II. The Bible Is a Book of Religion

The Bible lays no claim to being a book of history, science, or literature. It does not tell men all that they want to know, but it does tell them all they need to know. It is the written record of God's will for man. Of it Daniel Webster said, "The Bible is a book of faith, and a book of doctrine, and a book of morals, and a book of religion, of special revelation from God."

1. Redemption.—The Bible speaks of redemption. The Bible is designed to bring sinful man back to God. Therefore, it tells of man's creation and fall and the way of his restoration to fellowship with God. From Genesis through Revelation runs the scarlet trail of the Lamb slain before the world was created. The Bible tells of God's hatred for sin (Rom. 1:18) and love for the sinner (Gal. 1:3–4). It tells of man's futile efforts at salvation and his failure. It relates the incarnation of God in human flesh that he might be both "just, and the justifier of him which believeth in Jesus" (Rom. 3:26). It is God's written Word about the Word made flesh to dwell among us (John 1:14), of his birth, life, death, resurrection, continued intercession, and second coming. It tells of his Holy Spirit, who empowers and guides in God's redemptive mission (Matt. 28:19–20; Luke 24:49; Acts 1:8).

The Bible relates God's redemptive purpose in human history. It tells of God's choice of a man (Gen. 12:1 ff.); of a nation (Ex. 19:1 ff.); of the incarnation of God in his redemptive work (John 1:1–14); and through Jesus his choice of a people (Matt. 21; 1 Peter 2:4–10) by whom his gospel of redemption would be preached to the whole world until the end of the age (Matt. 28:19–20). It promises victory for his messengers as the conditions of Eden (Gen. 3) are restored (Rev. 22).

2. Judgment.—The Bible speaks of judgment. The principle of judgment runs all through the Bible. It tells of the judgment of Adam and Eve (Gen. 3:16–19), of Cain (Gen. 4:10–12), and of Noah's generation (Gen. 6). From it thunders God's judgment upon the Egyptians (Ex. 7–12). It speaks of God's judgment of Moses (Num. 20:11–12) and of David (2 Sam. 12:10–12). It does not overlook the judgment of Israel (Isa. 5) and of the nations (Amos).

While the Bible woos the sinner, it declares God's judgment against sin (Rom. 1:14–15). Men and nations stand or fall by its precepts and examples (Matt. 25:31–46). "Righteousness exalteth a nation: but sin is a reproach to any people [to a nation]" (Prov. 14:34). The Bible points to a final judgment for all (Rev. 20:11–15). "We shall all stand before the judgment seat of Christ" (Rom. 14:10).

3. *Duty.*—The Bible speaks of Christian duty. The Bible is a lamp unto our feet and a light unto our path (Psalm 119:105). "All scripture . . . is profitable for doctrine [teaching], for reproof, for correction, for instruction in righteousness: that the man of God may be perfect, throughly furnished unto all good works" (2 Tim. 3:16–17).

The Sermon on the Mount (Matt. 5–7) is the constitution of the kingdom of God. It is not designed to tell lost men how to be saved but to teach saved men how to live the Christian life. The Bible says much about good works, not as a means to salvation, but as instruction in how to show salvation through fruitful living (John 15; Rom. 6, 12; 1 Cor. 12–13).

III. The Bible Is a Book of Authority

All the Bible is the Word of God. While it was progressively revealed so that there is a higher concept of God in John than in Genesis, it is all the revelation of God to men. Progressive revelation does not refer to God's inability to reveal but to man's inability to receive the revelation (John 16:12–13). A teacher's gradual unfolding of truth is due to the pupil's limit of understanding, not the lack of the teacher's knowledge.

Only that Scripture which is fulfilled in Jesus Christ (the Levitical law of sacrifice) may be regarded as less binding on the Christian (Rev. 22:18–19). Since this is true, the New Testament is the Christian's only creed. But we must remember that Jesus authenticated the Old Testament as he gave the New Testament. The Bible, therefore, is the authoritative Word of God (Matt. 5:17–19, 27–48; 7:26–29).

1. Accuracy.—The Bible is historically accurate. In the field of ancient classics ten or fifteen manuscripts of any one work is regarded as a goodly number, sufficient to furnish an adequate study of its teachings. The number of manuscripts of the Bible in whole or in part runs into the thousands. Some of them date back to the fourth and fifth centuries A.D. By comparing them, going from the more recent to the oldest, it is possible to approximate the exact text of the originals. The recently discovered Dead Sea Scrolls (dated at least before A.D. 70) contained a complete copy of Isaiah.

However, the important thing is not merely to count these manuscripts but to weigh their value. At one time many of the critics of the Bible doubted the authenticity of many books of the Bible. But today few voices are heard in this regard. One by one the books of the Bible have stood the test of careful scrutiny. In 1809 Thomas Paine prophesied that in one hundred years the only Bibles would be found in museums. Today the Bible is the most widely circulated book in history.

One of the most serious charges once hurled at the Bible was that it was not historically trustworthy. At that time it seemed that the Bible was doomed. But its friends—and some of its enemies—armed only with spades, have completely authenticated the Bible. Of hundreds of discoveries in archeology that throw light on the historical accuracy of the Bible, not one has gone against the Bible. Every one has substantiated it. A few examples will suffice for the purpose of showing the historical accuracy of the Bible.

Many critics denied the Mosaic authorship of the Pentateuch, the first five books of the Bible. This denial was based on the theory that Moses could not write. But archeology has shown that the Egyptians had a highly developed system of writing long before the time of Moses. In this light it is absurd to avow that Moses, who "was learned in all the wisdom of the Egyptians" (Acts 7:22), could not write.

But there is more positive proof that the Hebrews of the fourteenth century B.C. could write. In 1904–5 Sir Flinders Petrie discovered in the region of Mt. Sinai ancient copper mines which had been worked by Midianite and Edomite miners. In addition to many Egyptian hieroglyphics, there was found an alphabetical script, written probably by the miners themselves. This writing represents the oldest alphabetical script known to man. Near these mines were found the ruins of an Egyptian temple whose remains showed a definitely Hebrew type of worship. Moses spent forty years in the area of these mines. The natural assumption is that this Moses, learned in all the wisdom of the Egyptians, not only could write but commanded that the Israelites write also (Deut. 6:9). Furthermore, a similar alphabetical writing has been found on pottery at Lachish in Palestine, probably brought there by the Israelites under Joshua. Only the most rabid critic today would claim that Moses was not capable of writing the Pentateuch.

Suffice it to say that archeology has also authenticated the story of the fall of Jericho (Josh. 6). Hundreds of such instances could be cited with regard to the science of archeology's proving the authenticity of the Old Testament.

The same story is true of the New Testament. The critics, seeking to destroy belief in the deity of Jesus, attributed the writing of the Gospel of John to some unknown presbyter as late as A.D. 165—anything to date it beyond the lifetime of the apostle John! But a few years ago a fragment of John's Gospel, now in the John Rylands Library in Manchester, England, was discovered. All papyrologists agree that it dates from not later than A.D. 125. Two leading papyrologists date it in the last quarter of the first century, the exact time that conservative scholarship has insisted that the Gospel of John should be dated. Thus again the Bible has been authenticated.

Sir William Ramsey once insisted that Luke was wholly unreliable as a historian. But after years of study he wrote a classic book on Luke, declaring him to be a historian of the first rank. Even where Luke differed with the known records of the Roman Empire, he was found to be correct. One example will suffice: Acts 13 records the visit of Saul and Barnabas to Cyprus. Luke says that the ruler of Cyprus was Sergius Paulus, a proconsul *(anthupatos)*, that is, a ruler under the power of the Roman senate. Roman records indicated that only a propraetor, a ruler under the power of the emperor, ever was stationed on the island. So, said the critics, Luke was wrong! But archeologists have discovered on Cyprus coins with the inscription "Sergius Paulus, proconsul." Thus Luke was right and the critics wrong. So has it ever been.

2. *Scientific correctness.*—The Bible is scientifically correct. The Bible is not a book of science, but it is scientifically true. Its language is that of popular religious usage, but its truth is that of exact science.

With the rise of an infant science the Bible was put on the defensive. Science had one theory today and another tomorrow, and because the Bible did not adjust to each new theory with the deftness of a chameleon, it was read out of court. Thus evolution denied the story of creation. Physiology overruled the virgin birth. Every miracle was denied, and sin was described merely as a maladjustment. The universe was pictured as a soulless machine. In return, theology adopted an attitude of dogmatism, describing science as a child of Satan.

But gradually the issue has moderated. Science became more reverent and theology less dogmatic. Today both, in large measure, are handmaidens of the Lord (see chapters 2–4). The more science learns, the nearer it gravitates toward biblical truth. The things it once denied it now either affirms or merely makes a point of inquiry. The material miracles of science make more plausible the divine miracles of the Bible.

In this atomic age scientists have become the most eloquent preachers of righteousness in the face of impending judgment. A few years ago a leading physicist described "In the beginning God" as the most eloquent words ever penned. From a recognition of God, science continues to gravitate toward a recognition of the Book of God. The Bible is unafraid. It can stand any test!

3. Experiential affirmation.—The Bible is experientially affirmed. The ultimate test of anything is that of experience. To say that the Bible is inspired of God; that it is infallible, without error, and trustworthy; that it is God's Word to man may sound to unbelieving hearts like just so many words. But experience no man can deny—if not his own, then that of others. The Bible has changed history and life as no other book has done. It changes the hearts of men. The Bible is its own best commentary and defense. If you read it, you will know that it is the Word of God, for it will speak to your heart of both God's love for you and your duty to him. Jesus said, you "search the scriptures; for in them ye think ye have eternal life: and they are they which testify of me. And ye will not come to me, that ye might have life" (John 5:39–40).

One of Billy Graham's aides tells of an old man in Germany who asked him to identify a printed page torn from a book. When told that it was from the Bible, the man replied, "I knew that it was something special, for nothing I ever read has affected me so."

2

Creation

*In the beginning God created the
heaven and the earth.* GENESIS 1:1

THE BASIC PROBLEM of human thought has
to do with the origin of the universe. This was the primary
question which occupied the Greek intellect. One of the first
Greeks to put his mind to this problem was Hesiod, who
wrote his *Theogony* in the eighth century B.C. Plato's *Timaeus* has aptly been called "the bible of Hellenistic cosmogony." From time immemorial men have been concerned
with how things came to be.

The problem of creation is one of cause and effect. Behind
each effect we look for a cause. In the study of nature we look
back from an effect to an immediate cause. Continuing this
process, we may expect to reach an effect which has no natural or visible cause. It is here that science runs into a blind
alley. Beyond this, science cannot go except by the leap of
faith. This Moses did when, six hundred years before Hesiod,
he wrote, "In the beginning God" (Gen. 1:1). The phrases

"blind alley" and "leap of faith" suggest several methods of approach.

I. The Methods of Approach

1. The approach of the mind.—This term is used to refer to those efforts to explain creation from the standpoint of material science and philosophy apart from revelation. This method has produced a variety of theories as to the origin of the universe. These may be listed briefly as (1) the atheistic theory; (2) the deistic theory; (3) the pantheistic theory. The atheistic theory rejects the idea of God altogether. This theory makes much of the law of continuity. It speaks of matter as eternal, with the resultant creation the product of pure chance or trial and error. It sees the universe as a great machine which grinds on in an endless process of evolution void of origin or end. The deistic theory says that if God created the universe, he wound it up like a vast machine, threw it out into space, and went off and left it to its own automatic working. Thus this answer sees the universe as impersonal. The pantheistic theory, largely the product of the philosopher Spinoza, teaches that God is identified with the universe, that God is one with matter and a prisoner within his own universe. All of these theories rule out the element of God's intervention in the working of the universe. Suffice it to say that those theories have long since been largely discarded by both science and religion.

2. The approach of the heart.—This term refers to those who insist upon revelation, according to their own understanding, as opposed to the mind or to science. From the beginning of the era of scientific investigation there has been war between theology and science. The scientist called the theologian a demagogue; the theologian regarded the scientist as a child of Satan. Both disregarded the other, reading the other's field out of the arena of consideration. Thus, as the scientist theorized in his pursuit of truth, the theologian dogmatized in his defense of the same. Unhappily, in this tug of war truth alone was the loser.

In this connection we might note Galileo's insistence that the earth revolves about the sun. So contrary was this idea to common belief and to that of the Church that it led to his inquisition in Rome and the forced renunciation of his teachings of the sun's being central in the universe.

The truth of the matter is that in the over-all struggle both science and theology have been wrong. Theology is nothing more than man's effort to rationalize God's biblical revelation; theoretical science is simply man's attempt to rationalize God's natural revelation. Men's efforts in both fields may conflict. But there is no conflict between true religion and true science, for both are of God.

3. *The approach of the heart and mind.*—This phrase refers to the combined approach both of religion and science. Theologians have not spoken their last word about God. Nor have scientists announced their last discovery in nature. But the more each comes to understand his own field in the light of the other, the greater the agreement with and understanding of the words of Moses, "In the beginning God created the heaven and the earth" (Gen. 1:1). "The theologian knows that God is Creator, but that fact does not tell him the *how* and *when*. The geologist knows the *how* and *when*, but the *Who* is a mystery to him. The Christian geologist, and the geologically minded theologian, alone can put together the *Who* of theology and the *what* of geology, and can show the connectedness between primary causation and secondary causation" (Ramm, pp. 226–27).

With the advent of Darwinism (from Charles Darwin's *The Origin of Species*, published in 1859 and his *The De-*

scent of Man, published in 1871) it seemed for a time that the theologian had had his day. But even in Darwin's day there were those who questioned the ability of science to speak authoritatively as to the ultimate in the creative record. With the turn of the century the pendulum of thought began to swing more toward the side of the theologian. Today, while there are voices to be heard on both extremes, the pendulum is more nearly in the center. The theologians have become more scientific, and the scientists have become more religious. Where the two have become wedded, they are producing the truth. Some leading scientists are now ardent Christians. While the union of these two branches of knowledge is not complete, they so approximate this position as to complement one another.

II. The Origin of the Universe

It should be remembered that the Bible is not a book of science. Therefore, we should not expect to find in it the language of the textbook. Instead, it uses that of religion at the popular level. It does not use the vocabulary of scientific investigation but that of personal observation. Thus Genesis 1 speaks not of solar systems but of that which may be observed with the natural eye. Yet the Bible is also the result of revelation; we may expect it to be in agreement with the proven facts of science. With this assumption let us examine the Genesis account of creation and other biblical references in the light of scientific theory and fact. "Genesis 1 now stands in higher repute than it could ever have stood in the history of science up to this point" (Ramm, p. 154). We shall assume that Genesis 2 is a specific account of certain elements contained in Genesis 1.

1. The time of "the beginning."—The widely accepted date of 4004 B.C. is the result of work done by Archbishop

James Ussher (1581–1656). Using the genealogical tables and other data in the Old Testament, he arrived at the above date. Lightfoot (1602–75), famed Hebrew scholar of Cambridge University, basing his work on that of Ussher, dated creation during the week of October 18–24, 4004 B.C., with the creation of Adam coming on October 23 at 9:00 A.M., forty-fifth meridian time (Ramm. p. 174)! However, Ussher's work was pure speculation prior to the modern age of geology and other related sciences. Archeology alone negates his theory.

The truth of the matter is that the Bible does not date the creation other than to say "in the beginning." Thus there need be no conflict between the biblical account and dates proposed by science. There is a conflict between Ussher and science, but not between Moses and science. Some insist that there is conflict between the various ages of science totaling billions of years and the seven days of Genesis. But we cannot be dogmatic. If we insist on a day's being twenty-four hours, there is an obvious conflict. But the Hebrew word for day (*yom*) is variously used for a twenty-four hour day (Gen. 8:4); a period of short duration (2 Kings 19:3; Psalm 20:1; Hab. 3:16); great events (Isa. 13:6; Jer. 46:10; Ezek. 30:3); and an unlimited period of time or an age (Isa. 65:2).

According to Genesis 1, it was the fourth day before God created the sun and moon "to divide the day from the night; and let them be for signs, and for seasons, and for days, and years" (Gen. 1:14). Note three different uses of the word "day" in Genesis 1 (vv. 5, 14). In Genesis 2:4 "day" refers to the whole period of creation. In view of the various uses of the word "day" listed above, it is clear that the various days of creation need not be regarded as of the same length. It is not a question of how much time God needed but of how much he chose to use. He could create the world in a million-eth of a second or in a million years. Time is no element with God (2 Peter 3:8).

2. *The cause of creation.*—With few exceptions the leading scientists of today hold to a theistic basis of creation—that is, that the cause back of creation is an intelligent being. Thus we may disregard atheism, deism, and pantheism. The standard proofs of God's existence (cosmological, teleological, anthropological, ontological, and moral, Mullins, pp. 124 ff.) may apply here. We note only the first two.

The cosmological proof simply infers that for the cosmos (universe) there must be a cause. Since pure material science must be silent here, we must depend upon revelation. Moses called the first cause "God." The teleological proof is an argument from design. The presence of design or order—that is, seasons, planetary movements, the atom—speaks for intelligence and purpose in creation. Neither a watch, a painting, nor a cyclotron can be explained as the product of mere chance. Infinitely more so can we not explain the universe as the product of blind chance or trial and error.

The teleogical argument is as old as the ancient Greeks and Hebrews. For a time modern science rejected it, but today many leading scientists are its strongest advocates. Sir James Jeans, leading English physicist, regards the Creator as a mathematician. Note the present-day emphasis upon mathematics as the key to the secrets of the universe.

Andrew M. Fairbairn says, "Whether mind may be conceived without matter, is a point that may be argued; but matter can be represented in no form which does not imply mind. . . . The highest speculations concerning the ultimate cause have been expressed in the terms of the intellect or the reason . . ." (*The Philosophy of the Christian Religion*, p. 49). He concludes, therefore, that "we cannot conceive either Nature or its creative work otherwise than through Mind. . . . To affirm the transcendence of thought is to affirm the priority of spirit, for spirit is but thought made concrete . . . and how can we better express this thought in its highest concrete form than by the ancient name of God?" (p. 55). It would seem that Genesis 1:1 agrees with this idea.

Furthermore, this is the message of revelation elsewhere. In John 1 Christ is presented as the Logos, a word which referred to the principle of divine reason. "In the beginning [cf. Gen. 1:1] was the Word [Logos], and the Word was with God, and the Word was God. The same was in the beginning with God. All things were made by him; and without him was not anything made that was made" (John 1:1-3). With this magnificent truth Paul agrees: "For by him were all things [the universe] created, . . . and he is before all things, and by him all things consist [hold together]" (Col. 1:16-17).

Recently a pastor told the author of hearing a scientist speak on Colossians 1:17. This scientist stated that the most unstable element known to science is the atom. Furthermore, said he, atomic scientists refer to the cohesive force of the atom as the "Colossian force."

3. The act of creation.—The Hebrew word meaning "to create" (*bara*) means to bring into being that which did not exist before (Heb. 11:3). From this idea comes the term "created *ex nihilo*," or created out of nothing. This does not teach the eternity of matter. Saying that nothing comes from nothing disregards the whole truth. Rational faith or spiritual reason sees something out of something or someone. Thus we are hemmed in to the recognition of a first cause whom we have identified as God. The word "create" is never used in the Bible apart from an activity of God. This does not mean that God is identical with his universe. Rather, it means that the universe is an outward expression of the will of God (Psalms 33:6; 148:5; 2 Peter 3:5).

4. The order of creation.—Before noting the *days* of creation let us note the primacy of water. Genesis 1:2 pictures water as covering the earth. Geology affirms this idea by saying that as the molten earth cooled, water would be formed. Turning to the days of creation, we note on the first day the appearance of light (Gen. 1:3–5). This light appeared before the appearance of the sun, moon, and stars (vv. 17–19). Some scientists have explained this as "cosmic light." One theologian calls it the "invasion of God" into the earth pattern.

On the second day there was the formation of the firmament or "limitless expanse" (vv. 6–8). Here was the division of water into earth water and atmospheric water. The power of God was revealed in the lifting of atmospheric water, the weight of which is said by scientists to be 54,460,000,000,000 tons. The weight of water is 773 times that of air (Smith, p. 317). This power of God is seen daily in evaporation. Science calls this time the pre-Paleozoic age. The important thing to note is not the difference between the exact language of science and the popular language of religion, but the coinciding of the order of events.

On the third day two events occurred: (1) the appearance of seas (plural) and dry land (vv. 9–10) and the arrival of plant life (vv. 11–12). Wilbur Smith (pp. 318–19) notes the word "earth" in three languages: *aretz* (Hebrew) means to break in pieces (crumbling); *chthōn* (Greek) means to bind to itself (gravity); *terra* (Latin) means to wear away (erosion). The Hebrew word, which antedates the others, suggests convulsions or earthquakes in nature such as the raising of the earth's surface in certain places with the attendant breaking up or crumbling of the planet to form mountains, valleys, and seas. This statement might in large measure have been lifted from a textbook in geology. Science agrees with the factors involved in all three of the above words.

There are only two, not three, varieties of plant life mentioned: grass and trees. The emphasis is on the method of reproduction: the one producing seed only; the other, fruit which contains the seed. Note that "after his kind" is used only twice. Botany affirms this.

The fourth day sees the appearance of the sun and moon (vv. 14–19). Some scientists, insisting that sunlight is necessary for plant life, object to this order, wherein the sun and moon appear after plant life. But note that in verse 16 it is not said that God created (*bara*) but that he made (*asah*). The word *asah*, according to one authority, also means to release from restraint. Thus God created the luminaries, as in verse 1. The sun was released from restraint on the fourth day in that its rays pierced the heavy mist surrounding the earth. But its unseen life-giving rays had been bombarding the planet from the first. It has also been noted that the planet Jupiter is still enveloped in such a mist so that the direct rays of the sun do not penetrate to the face of this planet, and so far as science knows, they never have. Jupiter, therefore, is called the "fourth-day planet."

To the fifth day is assigned the creation of marine and bird life (vv. 20–23). Science agrees that the first life on the earth appeared in water. The fact that the Bible adds birds to the list is significant when we compare their structure with that of the fish (Smith, p. 323). Both are egg-shaped with tapering bodies designed for swift movement. Both are suspended in the substance of their natural habitat: birds in the air, fish in the water. Both derive locomotion from fins or wings, finlike appendages. Both are covered with similar coatings growing out of their skins: birds with feathers, fish with scales.

Both have hollow, shell-like, light bones. Both are egg-layers. Both have oval-shaped blood corpuscles. Both are migratory in instinct.

On the sixth day was the creation of animals and man (vv. 24–28). Both science and the Bible agree that large animals and beasts (vv. 24–25) appeared on the earth just prior to man. Man was created separate and apart from all other of God's creatures (vv. 26–28). Of him alone does the Bible say that he was created in the image of God; that is, with a soul or spirit. With all other creatures there are many species—with man, only one (Acts 17:26–27).

The theory of evolution, or the law of continuity, is built upon guesswork alone. The so-called men, such as Neanderthal man, are built from sketchy bits of bone out of the imagination of men. The celebrated Piltdown man recently has been proved a hoax. There is not one bit of fact to substantiate the theory of evolution; it has been long since discarded by men of true science.

5. The object of creation.—The object of creation is the glory of God. "The heavens declare the glory of God; and the firmament sheweth his handywork" (Psalm 19:1).

III. The Lessons from Creation

1. Lessons about God.—Creation is the foundation of our knowledge of God, the triune God-Creator. It teaches the eternity of God—"in the beginning." It presents God [Elohim] in the plural of majesty, suggesting also the tri-unity of God (cf. "Let us make man," Gen. 1:26). In the creation we see God the Father (Gen. 1:1; Isa. 45:8,12); God the Son (John 1:3; Col. 1:16–17; Rev. 4:11); and God the Holy Spirit (Gen. 1:2).

2. Lesson about man.—Man is a created being made in the image of God. Seeing God as his creator, man is humble

(Psalm 8:3–4) ; has confidence that the God who made him can preserve him (Isa. 42:5 ff.) ; is brought to his knees in prayer to his Creator (Isa. 37:16) ; is brought low in worship (Ex. 20:8–11; Isa. 6:1–8) ; accepts his mission to have dominion over all creation (Gen. 1:28) and to evangelize the earth (Col. 1:15–23) ; and is inspired toward faith in God in all things (Psalm 90:1–2; Heb. 11:3) .

3. *Lesson of redemption.*—The fact of creation is the promise of our redemption. The Bible teaches that Christ died to redeem not only the souls of men (Eph. 2:10) but also the whole creation of God (Rom. 8:22; Rev. 21:1) . The real meaning of, "Behold, I make all things new" (Rev. 21:5) is, "Behold, I am re-creating all things." Blessed is the thought that he who spoke the universe into being can speak peace into the heart of every man!

3

God

Hear, O israel: the Lord [Jehovah] our
God [Elohim] is one Lord [Jehovah].
DEUTERONOMY 6:4

THE BELIEF IN THE EXISTENCE of God, or a divine being, is practically universal. The Bible does not argue the existence of God; it only declares his will and purpose. With only one statement the Bible dismisses the atheist: "The fool [unthinking person] hath said in his heart. There is no God" (Psalm 53:1). Note that he said in his heart; in his intellect he knew better. Anyone, like the psalmist, can look about him and see even in nature the evidence of God's existence and work (Psalm 19:1).

However, men's conceptions of God will differ. Many make God in their own image and according to their own desire. Others build their idea of God out of only one of his attributes—love, for example—to the neglect of all his other attributes. It is well, therefore, to see what the Bible says of him.

I. The Definition of God

E. Y. Mullins (pp. 214–15), leading Southern Baptist theologian, defined God in these words: "God is the supreme personal Spirit; perfect in all his attributes; who is the source, support, and end of the universe; who guides it according to the wise, righteous, and loving purpose revealed in Jesus Christ; who indwells in all things by his Holy Spirit, seeking ever to transform them according to his own will and bring them to the goal of his kingdom." In the Old Testament God is pictured in many ways: as a rock (Psalm 18:31, 46); a fortress (2 Sam. 22:2); a shield (Gen. 15:1); strength (1 Sam. 15:29); the mighty One (Gen. 49:24; Psalm 132:2, 5; Isa. 49:26); a husband (Jer. 31:32, cf. Hosea); a Father and Redeemer (Isa. 63:16); the Most High (Num. 24:16; Psalm 7:17); and the Holy One (Job 6:16; Isa. 29:23). We can, then, from this comprehensive definition and these descriptive thoughts derive much knowledge of God.

II. The Names of God

1. General names for God.—Many names in the Bible refer to him. *Elohim* (Gen. 1:1) is a plural word meaning God; it is a plural of majesty, whose root idea is energy or power. It means the "putter forth of power" or the One to whom all power belongs. It is found in the Old Testament 2,550 times. Usually it refers to God but is also used to signify pagan gods (1 Kings 18:21, 24; 2 Kings 1:2). The short form of this word is *El,* which is used in connection with other words to signify certain aspects of God: *El Shaddai,* God Almighty (Gen. 17:1); *El Elyon,* the most high God (Gen. 14:19); *El Olam,* the everlasting God (Gen. 21:33); *El*

Roi, "Thou God seest me" (Gen. 16:13). The Greek word corresponding to *Elohim* is *Theos.* (For this study of the names of God we are indebted to Stevenson, part one.)

Another name often used in the Bible for God is *Adonai* (Gen. 15:2, 8). It is a plural word meaning Lord. Sometimes it is used as a term of respect (Gen. 19:18) or to refer to the husband of a wife (Gen. 18:12). Used 340 times in the Old Testament, this word expresses the idea of personal relationship. It usually implies that God is a helper in time of need. Joshua called God *Adonai* following Israel's defeat at Ai (Josh. 7:10). Gideon received his commission from *Adonai* (Judg. 6:13,15). David confessed his sin to *Adonai* (2 Sam. 7:18; Psalm 35:23). In the temple following the death of King Uzziah, Isaiah "saw the Lord" [*Adonai,* who is identified as the Lord of Hosts (*Jehovah-sabaoth*)] (Isa. 6:1 ff.). *Adonai* is the Hebrew equivalent of the Greek word *kurios,* translated "Lord" with reference to Jesus. In both the Old and New testaments it was so used as the equivalent of *Jehovah.*

2. *The personal name for God.*—The name which identifies the God of the Hebrews as distinct from false gods (the god of the Moabites, Chemosh; of the Ammonites, Molech; of the Zidonians, Baal) is Jehovah or Yahweh. In English versions of the Old Testament it is translated by the word "Lord," except when used in connection with *Adonai* (Gen. 15:2) or *Yah,* a contraction of Yahweh (Isa. 26:4), when it is rendered "God" or "Jehovah." Appearing 6,823 times, it is the most popular name used for God. Many times it is used in conjunction with *Elohim* to point clearly to the fact that the God who did a thing was the true God (cf. Gen. 1:1; 2:3–4, 7).

The name Jehovah is also used in combination with other words to express various aspects of his person and work: *Je-*

hovah-sabaoth, Jehovah of Hosts or armies (1 Sam. 1:3);
Jehovah-jireh, Jehovah will provide (Gen. 22:14); *Je-hovah-rapha,* Jehovah that healeth (Ex. 15:26); *Jehovah-nissi,* Jehovah my banner (Ex. 17:15); *Jehovah-shalom,* Jehovah send peace (Judg. 6:24); *Jehovah-rohi,* Jehovah is my shepherd (Psalm 23:1); *Jehovah-tsidkenu,* Jehovah our righteousness (Jer. 23:6); *Jehovah-shammah,* Jehovah is there (Ezek. 48:35).

God definitely identified himself as Jehovah in speaking to Moses at the burning bush. He said, "I AM THAT I AM." Moses was to say to the children of Israel that "I AM hath sent me unto you" (Ex. 3:14). In Isaiah 42:8 ASV God said, "I am Jehovah, that is my name."

The name Jehovah comes from the Hebrew verb "to be" (*hayah*) and is a future tense in the third person singular, "He will be." In Hebrew the verb "to be" does not express the idea of eternal or absolute being. That concept is present in Jehovah only because it is the personal name of the God who is eternal. As such he is the eternal God who changes not (Isa. 57:15). He is the Creator (Gen. 2:4) and Sustainer of the universe.

In "I AM THAT [which] I AM" or "I WILL BE THAT [which] I WILL BE" (future tense, first person singular) Jehovah is identified not only by what he is but also by what he reveals himself as becoming. Previously, he had appeared to Abraham, Isaac, and Jacob as God Almighty (*El Shaddai*), "but by my name JEHOVAH was I not known to them" (Ex. 6:3). He appeared to them in his might. Here he reveals himself to Moses as redemptive love (Ex. 6:1–8). He is not only the eternal Creator or Sustainer of the universe and man, but in his redemptive will and work he reveals himself as becoming their Saviour.

Henceforth his revelation will be different: "There is no

God [Elohim] else beside me; a just God and a Saviour; there is none beside me. Look unto me, and be ye saved, all the ends of the earth" (Isa. 45:21–22). Here Jehovah revealed the unity of God, the righteousness of God, and the Saviourhood of God, not for the Israelites only but for the whole world. This verse might well be called the John 3:16 of the Old Testament. At this point it is well to note that the name Jesus (Jehoshua, or Yeshua) means "Jehovah is salvation."

Jehovah is a sacred name. "Thou shalt not take the name of Jehovah [actual meaning of "Lord" in the King James Version, here and elsewhere] thy God in vain" (Ex. 20:7, author's translation). Jesus taught us to pray, "Our Father which art in heaven, Hallowed be thy name" (Matt. 6:9). The name Jehovah was so revered by the Hebrews that they would not speak it, substituting the name *Adonai*. It was called the unmentionable name. Neither would they write it except with a new quill and new ink not previously used. If the Hebrews erred in one direction, we do so in the other. The name of the Deity is seldom heard from many lips except in profanity. "I am the Lord [Jehovah]: that is my name: and my glory will I not give to another, neither my praise to graven images" (Isa. 42:8).

III. The Person of God

God as he is revealed in the Bible is a person with all the qualities attributed to personality. Both the Scriptures and science agree that God is not a machine or a material manifestation but a person.

1. The unity of God's person.—We do not worship many gods. We worship one. "Hear, O Israel: the Lord our God [Elohim] is one Lord [Jehovah]" (Deut. 6:4). The unity of God expresses a denial of dualism, the theory that there exist a good and an evil principle of equal power, contending for mastery in the universe; and of polytheism, the theory that there are many gods. The theory that man began with the worship of many gods and finally evolved into the worship of one God has been proved false. In 1931 the sciences of archeology and anthropology simultaneously reached the conclusion that monotheism was the original religion of man (Marston, Chap. II). From this exalted concept of God man degenerated to polytheism (see chapter on Sin for treatment of Romans 1–3). Genesis and Deuteronomy 6:4 have been confirmed by science.

2. *The triune manifestation of God's person.*—The word "trinity" is not found in the Scriptures but was first used in the second century A.D. by Tertullian to express the truth taught in the Bible. The triunity of God was not discovered by man but revealed by God to man. The natural mind of man, endeavoring to express this idea of the manifold relations of God, made many idols (cf. Rom. 1–3). God revealed to man this idea of God's being one God with three relationships to man. Thus God is revealed in the Bible as God the Father (Gen. 1:1; Matt. 6:9); God the Son (Gen. 18:13; John 8:36); and God the Holy Spirit (Gen. 1:2; John 14:26). Note that all three manifestations of the Person of God are found in both Testaments. Whenever God appeared to men in bodily form, it was as the Second Person of the trinity (cf. Gen. 18:13; John 1:14). There is one exception: all three manifestations were present at the time of Jesus' baptism (Matt. 3:13–17).

It will help to understand this presence of the Trinity if we see history as a stage. In the Old Testament God the Father was in the center of the stage, with the Son and Holy Spirit in the wings. In the Gospels, God the Son is on stage, the Father and Spirit in the wings. In Acts and beyond, God the Holy Spirit is in the center of the stage, with the Father and

Son in the wings. All three manifestations of God are present at all times. It is a mystery beyond our comprehension.

Any illustration is inadequate, but a man in his family relationships might be used as an example. He is one person but bears the three relationships of father, son, and husband. In infinite degree God is Father (Matt. 6:9; John 17:1, 25); Son (Matt. 3:17; John 17:21); and Holy Spirit (Gen. 1:2; John 14:26; note especially Matt. 1:18–20).

3. The spiritual nature of God's person.—In John 4:24 Jesus said, "God is a Spirit: and they that worship him must worship him in spirit and in truth." As such God does not have a body; he is not material nor limited as is matter. While the Bible speaks of God as having hands, feet, arms, mouth, eyes, and wings, these are only anthropomorphic adaptations to enable us to understand God. To make our understanding clearer, we have the incarnation of God in Jesus (John 1:14; 14:9).

IV. The Attributes of God (Mullins, pp. 222 ff.)

By attribute we mean a quality ascribed to a person to describe his character or nature. The attributes of God are usually divided into the natural and moral attributes. Of course, all of God's attributes are moral and are natural to him, but for practical purposes we regard those as natural which apply to God's nature, and those as moral which apply to his character.

1. The seven natural attributes of God.—God is self-existent. God did not derive his being from any source outside himself. He did not will himself into being but exists by reason of what he is within himself (Gen. 1:1). He inhabits eternity (Isa. 57:15).

God is immutable. God does not change his character, nature, or purpose (Heb. 13:8; Mal. 3:6). This does not imply inactivity, lack of progress, lack of freedom to make choices, or inability to feel joy or sorrow. Nor does it mean that God cannot change his method in achieving his purpose. As music may be played with variations yet with the tune running through it, so God may express his immutable self-consistency in an endless variation of method (Num. 14:30–31; Deut. 32; Jer. 31:31–34).

Though God may change his procedure in view of the frailty of man, he does not change in his hatred for sin (Isa. 61:8; Jer. 44:4; Amos 5:21; 6:8; Zech. 8:17); his love of man (Hos.; John 3:16); or his redemptive will and purpose. When Israel refused to be a "kingdom of priests," God raised up another people through whom to express his will (Matt. 21; 2 Peter 2:5–10).

God is omnipresent. God is not confined to any part of his universe but is present in all his power at every point of space and in every moment of time (Psalm 139:7–12; cf. Holy Spirit). Thus God is not a tribal or national God but the God of all the earth (Gen. 18:25). He is the same God in Genesis that he is in John; only his method of revelation is different. He is the God of heaven, earth, and hell.

God is immense. God is superior to space. He is not confined to or limited by space (Isa. 57:15). He is not subject to the laws of space. God is not merely the God of the earth but of the universe (Gen. 1:1). No concept of man can contain him (Rom. 11:33–36; Luke 24:31–37; John 20:19).

God is eternal. Eternity refers to God's relation to time. Past, present, and future are equally known to him (2 Peter 3:8; Rev. 1:8). Time is like a parade which man, standing on the curb, sees a segment at a time—past, present, and future—but which God in a skyscraper at the end of the street sees all at one sweeping glance. Note Moffatt's translation of Jehovah as the Eternal (Psalm 23:1).

God is omniscient. Omniscience pictures the knowledge of God. It means that he has all knowledge (Job 38–39; Rom. 11:33–36) . Because God is everywhere at one and the same time, both in time and space, he knows everything simultaneously. But his foreknowledge of an event does not predetermine it. Man is a free moral agent, a personality, and though God knows in advance his actions, man is free to choose. The only responsibility God bears is that he does not prevent a man's action. But God works in all things for good to those who love him and fit into his unchanging purpose (Rom. 8:28) . God knew that Judas would betray Jesus; he did not force this action but used it to effect salvation. Further, God knows who will be saved and who will be lost. But his foreknowledge does not mean that he has arbitrarily named some for heaven and others for hell. Man still has the privilege of choice (see also the chapter on election) .

Finally, God is omnipotent. Omnipotence expresses the unlimited power of God to do anything that is not inconsistent with his nature, character, and purpose (Gen. 17:1; 18:14) . The only limitations on God's power are self-imposed (Gen. 18:25) . He cannot act in a manner that is inconsistent with his nature and purpose (Rom. 3:26) . Nor can he violate the laws of the universe. Miracles are in keeping with his laws about which we do not know.

A miracle is an event which occurs contrary to the laws of nature as we understand them. In the miraculous God does not set aside the laws of nature. He merely imposes upon them other laws unknown to us. Note the law of gravity and the law of aerodynamics. Even in redemption, over the moral law that the wages of sin is death God superimposes the spiritual law of his grace.

God cannot lie or make wrong to be right. He cannot undo what has been done. He cannot abolish the law of mathematics so that two plus two equals five. All these limitations are not defects but evidences of his perfection or omnipotence.

2. *The four moral attributes of God.*—God is holy. Holiness, according to Mullins (p. 230) , is God's "supreme moral excellence in virtue of which all other moral attributes have their ground in him. Holiness may be defined as the sum of other moral qualities, or perhaps better still, as their source and ground." The word "holy" comes from a root word which means to cut off, to separate, and hence to exalt. Thus it speaks of God as separated from or exalted above other things (Isa. 6:1–3) . The word originally contained no moral meaning. Things or people were holy even when dedicated to the service of immoral gods. As the word came to be used of Jehovah, it took on his moral excellence. Thus the holiness of God means simply his divinity or divine acts (Ex. 15:11,13, 17; Psalm 89:18; Hos. 11:9; Isa. 43:15; Heb. 3:3) . Things or people dedicated to God were regarded as holy. "Ye shall be holy, for I am holy" (Lev. 11:44; 20:26; Deut. 28:9–10. See also the chapter on salvation) . The holiness of God is involved in all of his other moral attributes.

God is righteous. Righteousness as applied to God refers to the self-affirmation of God on behalf of the right as opposed to the wrong. His righteousness is threefold: mandatory, with reference to the moral laws laid down to guide the conduct of men (as in the Ten Commandments) ; punitive, as seen in his administering of justice (Gen. 18:25; Deut. 32:4; Rom. 2:6–16) ; and redemptive, as revealed in his redemptive activity for man (Isa. 41:2; 43:1–6; 51:5) . In the New Testament this attribute is identified with the saving ministry of Christ (Rom. 1:17; 3:26; 6:23; 2 Cor. 5:21; 1 John 1:9; 2:1–2) . In the book of Romans the righteousness of God is an activity of God, growing out of his attribute as righteous, whereby he picks a man up out of unrighteousness and places him in a state of righteousness as though he had never been unrighteous (1:16–17; 3:24–26).

God is love. "Love may be defined as the self-imparting quality in the divine nature which leads God to seek the highest good and the most complete possession of his creatures. Love in its highest form is a relation between intelligent, moral, and free beings. God's love to man seeks to awaken a responsive love of man to God. In its final form love between God and man will mean their complete and unrestrained self-giving to each other, and the complete possession of each by the other" (Mullins, p. 236; 1 John 4:7–10). God is a jealous God (Ex. 20:5; Hos. 2:19).

God is truth. Truth means that he is "the source and ground of all forms of knowing, and all objects of knowledge" (Mullins, p. 240). This attribute arises out of his very nature (Ex. 34:6; Deut. 32:4). He is the basis of all human knowledge (Rom. 11:33–36). If we reject God, we lose all criteria of truth (Isa. 38:18). All spheres of truth—natural, physical, and religious—are grounded in God. For that reason there can be no conflict between true knowledge on these various levels of being. Theoretical science and theology may conflict since they are only man's attempts to rationalize these phenomena. But true science and true religion cannot clash, for both flow from the same source of truth—God (John 17:17). Mullins says, "Error in thought or speech is departure from reality in the constitution of man or nature or God" (p. 242; 1 Cor. 2). In Jesus Christ we have the incarnation of truth (John 1:14, 17; 14:6). In him are all the "treasures of wisdom and knowledge" (Col. 2:3).

V. The Fatherhood of God

1. The Old Testament picture.—It dimly suggests the fatherhood of God. He is a father to the fatherless (Psalm

68:5). His pity is likened to that of a father (Psalm 103:13). He is a father to Israel (Jer. 31:9). As a father he is dishonored by his children (Mal. 1:6).

2. *The New Testament portrait.*—The fatherhood of God is taught most clearly by Jesus. His relation to God as Son is abundantly seen (Matt. 11:25–26; 28:19; Luke 22:42; 23:34, 46: John 1:18; 3:35; 6:44–45; 10:38; 14:9; 17:21; note especially John 14–17). Furthermore, God is the father of all redeemed souls. God is the creator of all men, but he is father only to his children through Christ (John 1:12). Nowhere does the Bible teach the universal fatherhood of God and brotherhood of man. Old Testament references to God as father are directed to Israel only (cf. Mal. 2:10). In sin they are likened to the children of another (Ezek. 16:3, 45).

As our father, God is intimately acquainted with and associated with his children. The Bible knows nothing of deism, the philosophy which says that God created the universe but is absent from it and cares nothing about it. As father, God is concerned with our welfare (Matt. 6:25–34). As father, God invites us to pray to him (Matt. 6:5–15; Rom. 8:15). As father, God punishes or corrects his children (Heb. 12:5–11), but as father he forgives (Matt. 18:14; Luke 6:36) and comforts his children (2 Thess. 2:16). As father God delights to give good gifts to his children (Matt. 7:11; Rom. 6:23*b*).

3. *The significance of the fatherhood of God.*—As God's children we are to trust God (John 3:16); serve him (Matt. 5:16, 45); strive to be like him (Matt. 5:48); and glorify him (Rom. 16:25–27). As God's children we are heirs of all that he is and has. "Ye have received the Spirit of adoption [that is, the new birth, John 3:3–8], whereby we cry, Abba, Father. The Spirit itself beareth witness with our spirit, that we are the children of God: and if children, then heirs; heirs of God,

and joint-heirs with Christ; if so be that we suffer with him, that we may be also glorified together" (Rom. 8:15–17) . For "eye hath not seen, nor ear heard, neither have entered into the heart of man, the things which God hath prepared for them that love him" (1 Cor. 2:9) .

4

Jesus Christ

> *For God, who commanded the light to shine out of darkness, hath shined in our hearts, to give the light of the knowledge of the glory of God in the face of Jesus Christ.*   2 CORINTHIANS 4:6

JESUS CHRIST IS THE KEY to our knowledge of God and of history. The Bible itself becomes unintelligible apart from him. The Old Testament theme is the messianic hope. The Gospels recount his incarnation; Acts tells of his continuing work; the Epistles interpret his person and work; the Revelation sets forth his final victory and glory.

It is impossible for us fully to comprehend God until we grasp the meaning of the person and work of Jesus Christ. Only in considering him does history become more than frustration or, to borrow Shakespeare's description of life, more than a "tale told by an idiot, full of sound and fury, signifying nothing." It is of supreme importance, therefore, that we consider Jesus Christ.

I. The Names Accorded to Him

There are no less than eighty—and perhaps more—names given in the Bible to set forth Christ's person, nature, and work. Herbert F. Stevenson sets these forth at great length (pp. 101–61). Some ideas may be gained by a glimpse at a few of them.

1. The general names.—Christ is called the seed of the woman (Gen. 3:15); Shiloh, "he whose right it is" (Gen. 49:10); Branch of Jehovah (Isa. 4:2); Immanuel, "God with us" (Isa. 7:14); Wonderful Counsellor, mighty God, everlasting Father, Prince of Peace (Isa. 9:6); servant of Jehovah (Isa. 42:1); Rabbi, "teacher" (John 1:38; 3:2; 4:31; 9:2; 11:8); Rabboni, "my Teacher" (John 20:16); Teacher (Matt. 8:19; Mark 5:35; Luke 22:11; John 11:28); He that should come (Luke 7:19); Judge (John 5:27); Saviour (Luke 2:11); Lamb of God (John 1:29); Second Adam (1 Cor. 15:45); and Alpha and Omega (Rev. 1:11). A study of these will show their peculiar relation to the ministry of Jesus.

2. The specific names.—He is called Jesus. This name means "Jehovah is salvation" (Matt. 1:21). It is the Greek equivalent of the Hebrew word "Joshua" or "Yeshua." It is the name most frequently used in the Gospels and was a common name among the Jews. Jesus is the human and personal name given to our Lord and signifies that God has come to man in human form for his salvation. Hence "there is none other name under heaven given among men, whereby we must be saved" (Acts 4:12).

He is also called Christ. This is our Lord's official title. It is the Greek synonym (*Christos*) for the Hebrew word "Messiah," meaning the Anointed One, which sums up all the Jewish expectations of the Coming One (Luke 7:19).

The angelic host sang of him by this name at his birth (Luke 2:11). He assumed it at the beginning of his ministry (Luke 4:18). Peter later declared that "God anointed Jesus of Nazareth with the Holy Ghost" (Acts 10:38). Specifically Peter declared Jesus to be "the Christ, the Son of the living God" (Matt. 16:16). Thus the title Christ became a synonym for deity.

Jesus never used this title in reference to himself, but he did allow it with approval (Matt. 16:17). In Matthew 26:63–64 he admitted under oath that he was "the Christ, the Son of God." "Thou hast said" was in reply to a question which in Greek invites an affirmative answer.

Furthermore, Jesus is called Lord. Basically this word means owner, lord, or master with respect to slaves or property (Matt. 25:19). It is also a title of respect, like the English "sir" (John 20:15; Acts 9:5). In the Greek version of the Old Testament *Adonai* and Jehovah are translated as Lord. This title was given to Jesus at his birth (Luke 2:11) and was later applied to him by John the Baptist (Luke 3:4). In both these references the word clearly signifies Jehovah.

With the disciples it first included the idea of "master" but gradually took on its present meaning, as seen in Thomas' confession, "My Lord and my God" (John 20:28). Here and hereafter it contains for believers the full meaning of Jehovah (cf. 1 Peter 3:15; Isa. 8:13).

In the Epistles we find such combinations as "Lord Jesus Christ" (1 Cor. 16:22), "Jesus Christ our Lord" (Rom. 1:3); and "Lord Jesus" (1 Cor. 11:23). It is significant to note that this was a careful selection of names and order to show which aspect of Jesus' work was uppermost in the apostle's mind.

There were yet other specific names given to Jesus. He was called Logos or Word. This title refers to our Lord as the revealer of the Godhead (John 1:1). In time past God had spoken through prophets, but in the Logos he spoke through his son (Heb. 1:1–2). The term "Logos" was used by Greek philosophers to refer to the principle which controls the universe or the soul of the world. Philo, the Jewish Alexandrian philosopher, used it similarly with veiled reference to the Messiah. Logos was the Greek equivalent of the Hebrew word *memra,* used in the Targums to refer to the manifestation of God like the angel of Jehovah (Gen. 16:7) and the wisdom of God (Prov. 8). Thus in the term "Logos" John found a name for Christ which was already familiar to his contemporaries. His use of Logos was largely Hebrew in background, but to it he gave a distinctly Christian content. The Word was incarnate in Jesus (John 1:14).

The favorite name used by Jesus for himself was Son of man. It suggests his identity with man for man's redemption. It is not found in the New Testament, except when his questioners quoted his words, on any lips but his own (cf. Matt. 8:2; 9:6; 11:19; 12:8, 40: 13:41, 16:13; Mark 10:33; Luke 19:10; John 3:14; and many others) except in Stephen's vision of the glorified Christ (Acts 7:56). Ezekiel used this phrase ninety times but always in reference to himself. Its use by Jesus probably came from Daniel 7:13, where the prophet described a vision of successive world empires. After their fall there appeared one "like the Son of man" to receive his kingdom, which was quite unlike the earthly empires. Note that "Son of man" does not occur after the Gospels, except in Acts 7:56, until Revelation 1:13, where Christ appears as dwelling in his churches (cf. Eph. 1:22–23).

But Jesus is also called the Son of God. In the Old Testament "sons of God" is used to refer to men (Hos. 1:10) and angels (Gen. 6:2; Job 1:6). But in the New Testament "Son of God" refers to Jesus (Luke 1:32). Our Lord often used it of himself (John 3:16–17; Matt. 11:27). Peter used it with reference to Jesus (Matt. 16:16). But such a title and its cognates were used in direct address to him only by demons (Mark 5:7; Luke 4:41; Stevenson, pp. 123 ff.). Under oath Jesus admitted that he was the Son of God (Matt. 26:63–64).

II. The Pre-existence of Christ

1. The eternity of Christ.—That Jesus was the eternal Christ is seen in his genealogy. Luke takes his genealogy of Jesus back to "the son of Adam, which was the Son of God" (Luke 3:38). It is also seen in the prologue of John's Gospel. "In the beginning was the Word, and the Word was with God, and the Word was God. The same was in the beginning with God" (1:1–2). Note the use of "in the beginning" as in Genesis 1:1. In John 8:58 Jesus said, "Before Abraham was, I am." "Was" translates a Greek verb referring to becoming or being born. "Am" renders another verb, like our verb "to be," which refers to existence with no reference to origin. Thus Jesus said, "Before Abraham was born, I always have been." (See Hobbs, *Who Is This?* pp. 17–34, for a longer discussion of the pre-existence of Jesus Christ and other aspects of his person and work covered only briefly in this study.)

Further, the pre-existence of Christ is stated in Paul's Colossian letter: "the firstborn of every creature: . . . and he is before all things" (1:15–17). In this verse "all things" translates a Greek word meaning universe. Hebrews 13:8 describes Jesus as "Jesus Christ the same yesterday, and to day, and for ever." Furthermore, Jesus states it in Revelation: "I am Alpha and Omega, the first and the last" (1:11).

2. The creative activity of Christ.—Since God created by his spoken word, the Logos, Jesus is the creator (John 1:3–4; Col. 1:15–17; Rev. 4:11; cf. chapter 2). In his redemptive work he is re-creating all things (Eph. 2:10; Rev. 21:5).

3. The sustaining work of Christ.—He is the sustainer of the universe. "By him all things consist [hold together]" (Col. 1:17). Our universe is not a heliocentric but a Christo-centric universe.

III. The Incarnation of Christ in Jesus

The word "incarnation" means in flesh. In his incarnation, Christ, the Second Person of the Trinity, "was made flesh, and dwelt among us" (John 1:14).

1. The human side of the incarnation.—Jesus was fully man. It is as great a theological error to deny his humanity as to deny his deity. If the last generation battled to preserve belief in the latter, it is the present generation's duty to affirm the former, for only as truly man could Jesus be one with man. This truth is plentifully attested in the Gospels and Epistles. Jesus grew in wisdom and stature (Luke 2:52). He had limited knowledge (Mark 6:6; 13:32). He became tired and hungry (John 4:6; Matt. 4:2; Luke 8:23 ff.). He endured physical pain (Heb. 5:8) and felt human sorrow (Matt. 26:37; Mark 14:34; Luke 19:41; John 11:35). He was tempted (Matt. 4:1; Heb. 2:18) but was without sin (Heb. 4:15), and was subject to death (Matt. 27:50; Rom. 5:6).

2. The divine side of the incarnation.—But we must not forget that Jesus was fully God. Those who deny that Jesus claimed to be the Son of God must do so in the face of the Gospel records. He claimed to be one with God (John 10:30; 14:9). He exercised the power of God over nature (Luke 9:24 ff.; John 6:11 ff.); he healed the sick (Luke 17:12 ff.), raised the dead (John 11), and forgave sin (Mark 2:5). His enemies killed him "because he made himself the Son of God" (John 19:7). Without protest he allowed himself to be called God (John 20:28).

3. The divine-human element in the incarnation.—We

cannot understand the divine-human element in the incarnation of Jesus as the God-Man. Neither his friends nor enemies did so (Luke 8:25; John 6:52, 60; 19:7). The incarnation is a mystery beyond human comprehension (Eph. 3:4–12).

It is well to note that when Christ "emptied himself" (Phil. 2:6–11) he did not lose any of his deity. The Scripture here simply means that he put aside the "form of God" and took up the "form of a servant, and was made in the likeness of men." It is the picture of pouring the same amount of water from a round glass into a square glass. Christ lost nothing of his substance but changed only its form, shape, or manner of manifestation. Mullins gives three illustrations (p. 185): a mathematical genius teaches a beginner while retaining all his mathematical knowledge; a musical genius at a given time and for sufficient reason may play the piano while wearing gloves; a department store magnate drops from his consciousness all his knowledge of a great chain of stores to minister to a seriously injured son.

G. Campbell Morgan speaks of the incarnation as the wick of Christ's deity being turned down. At the transfiguration the light which shone from Jesus was the wick of his deity turned up. Campbell also makes this suggest Christ's sinlessness. If there had been a flaw in his character, this deity would have destroyed him as a lamp chimney with a crack in it is shattered by inrushing of heat when the wick is suddenly turned up.

IV. The Evidences of Jesus' Deity

1. The virgin birth of Jesus.—The virgin birth was foreseen at the very gates of Eden (Gen. 3:15) and was foretold by the prophet (Isa. 7:14; cf. Matt. 1:22–23.). Mark is silent on this point because he begins his record with the public ministry of Jesus (1:1 ff.). John does not record it because it was already fully told in previous Gospels (Matthew and Luke, but cf. 1:14). Paul, while not plainly affirming the virgin birth, implies it (Gal. 4:4). No question was raised about it in Christian history, except by Jesus' enemies (John 8:41), until the eighteenth or nineteenth century. There were many people alive when the Gospels were written, including Mary, who could have denied it if it had been untrue.

The virgin birth is fully recorded in two of the Gospels. Matthew records it when he says that Jesus was conceived by the Holy Spirit (1:18, 20). He is careful to avow it in his genealogy (1:16), even to the point of showing that Joseph knew that he was not Jesus' father (1:18–19).

Luke was a physician (Col. 4:14). His writings reveal the language of a first-rate physician such as were Galen and Hippocrates. As a scientist he knew how to find and weigh evidence. Luke spent two years in Palestine during Paul's imprisonment at Caesarea (Acts 23–26) during which time he carefully examined the gospel story. After "having had perfect understanding of all things from the very first [having traced all things accurately from the very first]" (Luke 1:1–3), he wrote his Gospel. As a physician Luke would enjoy the confidence of Mary.

All of Luke's training and experience would deny the possibility of a virgin birth. To record such an occurrence as a fact would subject him to great criticism. Yet the evidence was so conclusive that he gave the most complete story of the virgin birth of Jesus on record. Not once in demonstrable historic facts has Luke been proved in error. If we are to be scientific, we are compelled to accept his testimony as to the virgin birth of Jesus. The virgin birth is morally necessary (Gen. 3:15), divinely possible (Luke 1:37), authentically recorded (Luke 1:1–3), and experientially affirmed (John 3:16).

2. *The marvelous life of Jesus.*—There is further evidence of Jesus' deity in his life. Jesus was a perfect man (Heb. 4:15). His own enemies could find no fault in him (John 8:46; Luke 23:4; Matt. 27:4). Even those who deny the deity of Jesus testify to his goodness. But if Jesus were not what he claimed to be, he was not even good. He can be condemned with scant praise.

He taught as "never man spake" (John 7:46). His teachings were based not on the authority of others (Matt. 7:29; Mark 1:22) but upon his oneness with God (John 3:11; 7:16–17; 8:26). The word "authority" in these verses translates the Greek word *exousia,* which means "out of being." Jesus taught out of the very nature of his being. He taught about God (Luke 2:49; cf. Matt. 6:26–30; 16:1–3; John 3:8; 12:24). He taught about himself (Luke 4:18–21; John 6:35; 8:12; 10:2, 7; 11:25; 15:1). He taught about man; he knew the innermost workings of the mind and soul of men (John 2:25). He recognized the primacy of motive in conduct (Matt. 5:21–48; 23:25–28). He taught with a purpose (Matt. 7:24–29). His invitation was for men to enrol as his pupils (Matt. 11:29–30). The Lord's methods of teaching have never been excelled.

Jesus' wondrous works "manifested forth his glory" (John 2:11; 3:2) and showed that the Father had sent him (John 5:36). His disciples asked, "What manner of man is this, that even the wind and the sea obey him?" (Mark 4:41). John's Gospel is built about "signs" (2:11; "miracle" translates the Greek word *sēmeion,* which means "sign") of Jesus' deity "that ye might believe that Jesus is the Christ, the Son of God; and that believing ye might have life through his name" (John 20:31). Jesus ever sought to lead men from the outward miracle to its inward significance (John 6:26). He declared that his miracles would be the basis of judgment (Matt. 11:21–22.).

3. The resurrection of Jesus.—The crux of the evidence concerning Jesus' deity is seen in his resurrection. This was his greatest miracle. Repeatedly Jesus' enemies asked for a sign of his deity. Only one did he give: his resurrection (Matt. 12:39–40; 16:4; Luke 11:29–30). When it came to pass, they lied about it (Matt. 28:11–15). Though the Jews sealed the tomb and placed a guard before it, Jesus was "declared to be the Son of God with power . . . by the resurrection from the dead" (Rom. 1:4). God caused the enemies of Jesus to furnish the most certain proof of the deity of our Lord! Modern denials of the resurrection have served only to cause his followers to re-examine its many proofs that they might have many reasons for the faith that is within them (1 Peter 3:14–16).

V. The Significance of Jesus' Death, Resurrection, Ascension, and Second Coming

1. The meaning of Jesus' death.—At the cross are shown the deepest depth of sin and the highest level of the love of God.

Jesus' death was voluntary. He was the Lamb of God "slain from the foundation of the world" (Rev. 13:8). Six months before his crucifixion Jesus prophesied it (Matt. 16:21), and three days prior to it he fixed the exact day (Matt. 26:2). He came to give his life a ransom for many (Matt. 20:28) and refused to accept human aid (John 18:10–11) or to call for divine deliverance from it (Matt. 26:52–53). No man took his life from him, for he laid it down of himself (John 10:17). He even refused to die on the cross until all things for man's redemption had been finished, and then he "yielded up the ghost [dismissed his Spirit]" (Matt. 27:50). Jesus died not as a criminal but as a king (Matt. 27:37).

Furthermore, his death was vicarious or substitutionary. Following the raising of Lazarus, Caiaphas unwittingly pointed to the meaning of Jesus' death when he said, "It is expedient for us, that one man should die for the people" (John 11:50). "For" translates the Greek word *huper,* which means "instead of," "in place of," or "as a substitute for." It means to lay oneself across another to take a blow intended for him. "The wages of sin is death" (Rom. 6:23). Someone who is himself sinless must die for sin (2 Cor. 5:21). In his virgin birth and sinless life Jesus alone qualified. He justified the law of God and became the Lamb of God without spot or blemish (1 Peter 1:19). Through him, therefore, God could be both "just, and the justifier of him which believeth in Jesus" (Rom. 3:24–26; cf. Isa. 53:5–6; Gal. 3:13; 1 Peter 1:18–21; 2:24; 1 John 2:2).

Jesus' death was once for all. There is no need for another Saviour; there will be no other: "But now *once* [once for all] in the end of the world [age] hath he appeared to put away sin by the sacrifice of himself. . . . So Christ was *once* [once for all] offered to bear the sins of many" (Heb. 9:26, 28; author's italics).

2. The meaning of Jesus' resurrection.—Many men died on crosses. Had Jesus' ministry ended there, he would have been but another martyr to a cause. The Bible, however, records his resurrection. This is one of the best authenticated events in the history of the world. Efforts to explain away the resurrection of Jesus have fallen in upon themselves. The empty tomb has never been refuted or explained away. The historicity of Luke, along with other witnesses, stands as a bulwark of faith. Apart from the ten post-resurrection appearances of Jesus it is psychologically impossible to explain the faith of the early disciples or subsequent Christian history. The resurrection was the theme of first-century preaching (Rom. 1:4). Only those who could witness to the resurrection could be apostles (Acts 1:22). In no other way can the transformation of Saul into Paul (Acts 9) be accounted for.

Why is the resurrection of Jesus so vital to the gospel message? First, it proves the deity of Jesus Christ. The resurrection was our Lord's one "sign" of his deity given to his enemies (see above). Second, it makes effective Jesus' death. A dead Saviour would be no Saviour at all (1 Cor. 15:17). Paul said that Jesus was crucified for our sins and raised from the dead for our justification (Rom. 4:25). First Corinthians 15 is the fullest account of what the resurrection means to our salvation. Third, the resurrection fulfilled his promise for daily companionship in service. We do not serve a dead Jesus but a living Lord.

When Jesus gave the Great Commission (Matt. 28:19–20) he did so because "all power [authority]" had been given to him. "Power" translates the word *exousia,* "out of the very nature of being." As the resurrected Lord, Jesus made this direct claim to authority out of the very nature of his being. While he had claimed this for himself indirectly at other times (Matt. 9:6; 21:24; John 5:27; 10:18), here he majestically proclaimed that "all power" or authority had been given to him (cf. Rom. 1:4). As the risen Lord he promised to be with his followers always (Matt. 28:20). In trials they are assured of his concern (Acts 7:56; 9:4; 18:9–10; 27:23–24; 2 Tim. 4:17).

Fourth, the resurrection promises to believers a resurrection from the dead (cf. 1 Cor. 15). "For our conversation [citizenship] is in heaven; from whence also we look for the

Saviour, the Lord Jesus Christ: who shall change our vile body, that it may be fashioned like unto his glorious body" (Phil. 3:20–21). "Because I live, ye shall live also" (John 14:19).

3. The meaning of Jesus' ascension.—Forty days after his resurrection Jesus ascended into heaven from the Mount of Olives (Luke 24:50–51; Acts 1:9). There he was "highly exalted" (Phil. 2:9) as he bore his precious blood as evidence of his atonement (Heb. 9:12). Now he is seated at the "right hand of God; from *henceforth expecting till his enemies be made his footstool*" (Heb. 10:12–13; author's italics). In the meantime, he is the Christian's Advocate with the Father (1 John 2:1), making intercession for him (Heb. 7:25) that he might have forgiveness for sins (1 John 1:9).

4. The meaning of Jesus' second coming.—Before he went away Jesus promised repeatedly that he would return (Matt. 25:31; John 14:3; Acts 1:11). There is no more certain promise of God than this: "For the Lord himself shall descend from heaven with a shout, with the voice of the archangel, and with the trump of God" (1 Thess. 4:16). Then he shall put all enemies under his feet (1 Cor. 15:25–26; 50–57). Then will he be "KING OF KINGS, AND LORD OF LORDS" (Rev. 19:16). "He which testifieth these things saith, Surely I come quickly [suddenly]. Amen. Even so, come, Lord Jesus" (Rev. 22:20).

5

The Holy Spirit

But the Comforter, which is the Holy Ghost [Spirit], whom the Father will send in my name, he shall teach you all things, and bring all things to your remembrance, whatsoever I have said unto you. JOHN 14:26

THE HOLY SPIRIT is the Third Person of the Trinity. As God the Father (First Person) revealed himself in human form (Jesus, the Second Person), so he revealed himself in spiritual form as the Holy Spirit (Third Person). Thus there is one God, bearing three relationships to nature and man.

The Holy Spirit is the most neglected member of the Trinity. There are six reasons for this neglect. (1) The doctrine of the Holy Spirit is difficult to understand: "But the natural man receiveth not the things of the Spirit of God: . . . neither can he know them, because they are spiritually discerned" (1 Cor. 2:14). (2) The Holy Spirit is placed third

in the Trinity (Father, first; Son, second; Holy Spirit, third).
Thus we unknowingly relegate him to a place of unimportance. (3) There is also a tendency to refer to the Holy Spirit
as "it." To speak of a person as an "it" makes of him a nonentity. (4) Emotional excesses of some tend to defame the
Holy Spirit. (5) There is a fear of sin against the Holy Spirit.
For this reason men avoid him. (6) The use in the King
James Version of Holy Ghost is unfortunate. In A.D. 1611
ghost meant spirit; today it means the spirit of a dead person
or "hant."

For their neglect of the Holy Spirit, Christians pay a great
price in loss of spiritual power. It is important, therefore,
that they have a proper understanding of him.

I. Definition of Terms

1. Ruah.—The Hebrew word for spirit is *ruah,* which
meant, originally, "breath," later, "wind," and finally, "spirit."

2. Pneuma.—The Greek equivalent is *pneuma* (note the
English word "pneumatic"), with the same meaning of
breath, wind, or spirit. It is of interest to note the word
"wind" (*pneuma*) in John 3:8 and Acts 2:2. The word has
the idea of an intangible substance but one which has great
power either for constructive or destructive use according to
relationship to it.

3. Spirit.—The word "spirit" is always, in the Bible, associated with power or force. Note Genesis 1:2: "The Spirit
of God moved . . ."

4. Holy.—The word "holy" came to be associated with
Spirit as the title became related to God (Isa. 63:10).

II. The Holy Spirit in the Scriptures

The Holy Spirit is presented in both the Old Testament
and the New Testament (Mullins, pp. 203 ff.).

1. The Holy Spirit in the Old Testament.—The Holy Spirit was present in the creation of the natural universe (Gen. 1:2; Psalm 104:28–30). In Genesis 1:2 the word "moved" may also be translated "brooded," as in the sense of a mother hen's looking after her chicks. (Note Jesus' attitude toward men in Luke 13:34.) The Holy Spirit was also present in the creation of man: "Let us make man" (Gen. 1:26; 2:7). Furthermore, he was at work throughout the Old Testament. He came upon men who did great works for God (Judg. 11:29; 14:6). Wisdom and skill came from the Holy Spirit (Ex. 28:3; 31:2–5; 35:31). He endowed the prophets with wisdom and revealed divine truth to them (Ezek. 2:2; 8:3; 11:1, 24). He was present in men as an ethical force (Psalm 51:11; Isa. 63:10). He was to be the anointing power for the Messiah (Isa. 11:2; 61:1). A future outpouring of the Holy Spirit was promised (Joel 2:28–32).

2. The Holy Spirit in the New Testament.—The revelation of God as Holy Spirit is seen in its fulness in the New Testament. In the Gospels the Holy Spirit was the agent in the conception of Jesus (Matt. 1:18). He was present at Jesus' baptism (Matt. 3:16). He drove Jesus into the wilderness for his temptation (Matt. 4:1; Mark 1:12; Luke 4:1). After the temptation Jesus came to Galilee in the power of the Spirit (Luke 4:14). In the beginning of his public ministry Jesus declared that the "Spirit of the Lord" was upon him (Luke 4:16–21; cf. Isa. 61:1–2) to enable him to do his mighty works (Matt. 12:18, 31; Mark 3:28–29).

Jesus sent forth his disciples in the power of the Spirit of the Father (Matt. 10:16–20). He went to the cross in the "eternal Spirit" (Heb. 9:14). Before his death he promised the coming of the Holy Spirit in the Spirit's distinctive ministry (John 14:16–18). He was raised from the dead according to the Spirit of holiness (Rom. 1:4). After the resurrection he told his followers to wait in Jerusalem for the coming of the Holy Spirit upon them (Luke 24:49), after which they were to preach the gospel to the whole world, baptizing in the name of the Father, Son, and Holy Spirit (Matt. 28:19).

In Acts, the Epistles, and Revelation the Holy Spirit is presented as continuing his work. At Pentecost the Holy Spirit came upon the Christian group (Acts 2:1 ff.). The remainder of Acts is the record of the Spirit's work through the early church. Acts has been aptly called the "Gospel of the Holy Spirit." In the Epistles the Holy Spirit is seen bestowing gifts of power upon the early Christians (1 Cor. 12). Paul's concept of the Christian life involved at every point the presence and fellowship of the Holy Spirit as believers walk in the Spirit (Rom. 8:1) and were commanded not to grieve the Holy Spirit (Eph. 4:30).

Paul's preaching was "in demonstration of the Spirit and of power" (1 Cor. 2:4). Peter said that Christians are "quickened [made alive] by the Spirit" (1 Peter 3:18) and sanctified by him (1 Peter 1:2). According to Revelation, John was "in the Spirit on the Lord's day" (1:10). The last invitation in the Bible reads, "The Spirit and the bride [church] say, Come" (Rev. 22:17).

3. The personality of the Holy Spirit (cf. Turner, pp. 90–91).—It is important to remember that the Holy Spirit is a person. He is the Third Person or manifestation of the Godhead (Gen. 1:2; Matt. 3:16; 28:19). He is referred to not as "it" but as "he" (John 14:16–17, 26; 16:7 ff.). He does the work of a person: he testifies (John 15:26), reproves (John 16:8), comforts (John 14:16–18, 26), guides (John 16:13), strives (Gen. 6:3), and helps (Acts 1:8). The Holy Spirit reacts like a person. He may be resisted (Acts 7:51), grieved (Eph. 4:30), insulted (Heb. 10:29) ("done despite" means insulted), blasphemed (Matt. 12:31), received (John 20:22).

The Holy Spirit is God. He is not merely a person but the divine Person. Peter declared him as God when he accused Ananias of lying to the Holy Spirit, saying, "Thou hast not lied unto men, but unto God" (Acts 5:4). The Scriptures ascribe to him the attributes of God: omnipresence (Psalm 139:7); omniscience (1 Cor. 2:10); and omnipotence (1 Cor. 12:11). He does the work of God (Gen. 1:2; Luke 4:14; John 3:5; 16:8; Rom. 8:11).

But we can best understand the Holy Spirit as the "Other Jesus" (B. H. Carroll), or as Marcus Dods calls him, "Jesus' alter ego." Luke expressed this idea in the introduction to Acts when he spoke of "all that Jesus *began* both to do and teach" (1:1; author's italics). He then proceeded to relate what the Holy Spirit continued to do and teach. Jesus himself foresaw that his work would be continued when on the night before his death he promised that the Father would send the Holy Spirit: "I will not leave you comfortless [orphans]: I will come to you" (John 14:18). Henceforth the Holy Spirit would be to them all—and more—that Jesus had meant to them. As Jesus had worked with them, so the Holy Spirit would work through them. Jesus could only be in one place at one time; the Holy Spirit would be everywhere at the same time. As Jesus had taught them, so the Holy Spirit would teach them. Jesus was with them for only three and a half years in Palestine; the Holy Spirit would "abide with you for ever" (John 14:16), "even unto the end of the world [age]" (Matt. 28:20). The Holy Spirit would not testify of himself but of Jesus (John 15:26).

III. The Specific Work of the Holy Spirit

We have noted the work of the Holy Spirit in creation, in mighty works through Old Testament characters, and in the virgin conception of Jesus. In every aspect he appears as creative, operative, or generative power. All these are more fully seen in his specific work.

1. The Holy Spirit's work in regard to the Scriptures.— The Holy Spirit is active in revelation. The Holy Spirit revealed the will of God to men. Nothing is clearer than the truth that in given historical environments God reveals to men his truth, which is both timely and timeless. This revelation is given by the Holy Spirit who spoke through, for example, God-conscious prophets (Jer. 1:4 ff.; Ezek. 2:1 ff.; H s. 1:1–2; 4:1; Joel 1:1) ; Jesus (Luke 4:18) ; and the New Testament writers (Heb. 2:1–4; Rev. 1:10) . Furthermore, the Holy Spirit is the source of inspiration. Not only does he reveal the truth of God, but he inspires (breathes in) men to preach it and to write it for posterity: "For the prophecy came not in old time by the will of man: but holy men of God spake as they were moved [picked up and borne along] by the Holy Ghost [Spirit]" (2 Peter 1:21; cf. 2 Peter 3:2) . "All scripture is given by inspiration of God [God-breathed]" (2 Tim. 3:16) . "Moses wrote all the words of the Lord" (Ex. 24:4; Deut. 31:9) . The prophets were commanded to write their visions and messages (Isa. 30:8; Jer. 30:2; 36:1–2, 28; Ezek. 43:11; Heb. 2:2; cf. John 1:45) . As Paul wrote, he was conscious of the Lord's guidance (Rom. 1:1–7; 1 Cor. 11:23 ff.; Gal. 1:11–12) . The Revelation came to John as he was in the Spirit (Rev. 1:10) .

Again, the Holy Spirit was active in illumination. This term means the Holy Spirit's enlightenment of the minds and hearts of those who recorded and interpreted the gospel story. Jesus promised that the Holy Spirit would bring to their remembrance all his words and would teach them all things (John 14:26) . The things which Jesus wished to tell his disciples but which they were not prepared to understand would be told to them by the Holy Spirit. The Holy Spirit would not speak of himself but of Christ: "Whatsoever he shall hear, that shall he speak" (John 16:13). Thus through the Holy Spirit Jesus would complete his own interpretation of himself. This interpretation, which he began following the resurrection (Luke 24:25–27, 44–49), he would complete through the Holy Spirit. Furthermore, the Holy Spirit would show the disciples "things to come" (John 16:13; cf. Revelation). The Holy Spirit still guides the prayerful student of the Scriptures to an understanding of them.

2. *The Holy Spirit's work in administration.*—The Holy Spirit is the administrator of the kingdom of God. This truth we have seen in his work through men and women in the Old Testament. Even Jesus was anointed with the Spirit (Luke 4:18 ff.; Acts 10:38), was led by the Spirit (Matt. 4:1), and worked by the power of the Spirit (Luke 4:14; John 14:10). Because the Holy Spirit would come in power upon Jesus' followers, they would be able to do even greater works than Jesus himself did—not greater in kind but in scope (John 14:12–17). Through the Spirit present-day Christians are mysteriously identified with the Lord in his work (John 14:20–21). For that reason the early Christians, and we, must wait for the Holy Spirit's presence and power (Luke 24:49; Acts 1:8).

This work of administration is most clearly set forth in Acts, the Gospel of the Holy Spirit. He came in power at Pentecost, transforming the disciples from cowering rabbits into bold lions (Acts 2:4; 5:25–32). Their dealings were directly with God, the Holy Spirit (5:3–4). The Holy Spirit gave them words to speak before councils and critics (Matt. 10:19–20; Acts 6:10; 15:7). He was with them in their trials and persecutions (Acts 7:55 ff.). He encouraged them in their decisions (Acts 15:28). Every new development in the spread of the gospel in the book of Acts was under the guidance and with the approval of the Holy Spirit. Through the miracle of tongues he enabled the apostles to preach the gospel to Jews from all parts of the Roman Empire (2:6–18). The word translated "tongues" simply means languages. In order to hasten the spread of the gospel, the early Christians were enabled to speak languages other than their own without previous academic preparation. The word "unknown" (1 Cor. 14:2, 4) is in italics in the King James Version of the Bible; this indicates that it is not in the original Greek (read 1 Cor. 14:1–19). This gift of tongues was to be used to preach to people of other languages, not as a selfish display of personal spiritual gifts. No one was to speak in another tongue or language without an interpreter for those present who did not understand it. The New Testament knows nothing of the unknown tongues of certain modern groups!

The Holy Spirit approved the preaching of the gospel to half-Jews or Samaritans (Acts 8:15 ff.). He directed Philip to preach to a Jewish proselyte, the Ethiopian eunuch (8:26–40). He guided Cornelius and Peter (Acts 10) to bring the gospel to God-fearers (10:2), Gentiles who had studied the Jewish religion but had not yet accepted it, and approved their becoming Christians (10:44 to 11:18). The Holy Spirit led Barnabas and others to preach the gospel to Gentiles in Antioch (11:19–30). He ordered Barnabas and Saul sent forth as missionaries to the pagan people of Asia Minor (13:2 ff.). He guided Paul to Troas, where he gave Paul the vision calling him to Europe (16:6 ff.). He authenticated Paul's work in Ephesus (19:1 ff.). He inspired Paul to go to Jerusalem and then led him to go to Rome (19:21; 20:22–23; 27:23–24; 28:25 ff.).

The Holy Spirit inspired the writing and gathering of the New Testament into the canon of Scripture. He led in the spread of the gospel throughout Europe and America. He still guides the largest mission board, the smallest church, and the humblest Christian.

3. *The Holy Spirit's work with lost people.*—While the Holy Spirit administers the broad reaches of the program of the kingdom of God, he also works with individuals. Without his work ours would be in vain. His work with the lost is threefold. First, he works in conviction. Jesus said that the Holy Spirit would convict "the world of sin, and of righteousness, and of judgment: Of sin, because they believe not on me" (John 16:8–9). The Holy Spirit shows man the awfulness of sin and what it does, not merely to the sinner but to God. He brings man to realize that he is a sinner and that the greatest sin is unbelief in Jesus. "Of righteousness, because I go to my Father, and ye see me no more" (John 16:10). The Holy Spirit leads man to see that compared to Christ's righteousness his self-righteousness is as filthy rags (Isa. 64:6). Furthermore, he shows man the righteousness of God which is not by works but by faith in Jesus (Rom. 1:16–17). "Of judgment, because the prince of this world is judged" (John 16:11). Man is led to admit the righteous judgment of God upon him because of his sin. Thus he is ready to reject Christ and accept hell or to accept Christ and accept heaven.

It is well at this point to note briefly the sin against the Holy Spirit (Matt. 12:27–37). The Pharisees attributed the power of the Holy Spirit in Jesus' casting out demons to the devil. So fixed were they in their scorn of Jesus, the Son of God who worked by the Spirit of God, that they attributed his divine work to demonic powers. In so doing they blasphemed the Holy Spirit, by whom this power was made operative. In their persistent unbelief there was no hope for them.

The person who continues to reject the saving power of

God in Christ through the Holy Spirit is like them. He says that the salvation offered is not of the God of truth but is a deception of Satan. In the words given to Satan by John Milton, he says, "Evil, be thou my good." So crystallized is his attitude of unbelief that he cannot receive salvation. Men can live physically and yet be so hardened spiritually that they already cannot believe.

Men should beware of continued rejection of Christ. If they blaspheme or reject God the Father, there are still left the Son and Holy Spirit. If they blaspheme or reject the Son, there is still the Holy Spirit. If they blaspheme or reject the Holy Spirit—there is none other to whom they can turn. No Christian can commit this sin. The person who thinks that he has committed it has not, for the Holy Spirit is still convicting him of sin. But the lost person should beware, for God says, "My Spirit shall not always strive with man" (Gen. 6:3).

Furthermore, the Holy Spirit works in a person's believing on Jesus. He points the convicted sinner to Christ, his only hope, and enables him to turn to Christ in faith and trust. Of course, man must respond in faith. Either he will do so or else he will reject Christ. Again, the Holy Spirit produces the new birth. When man turns in faith to Jesus, by the mysterious process of regeneration he is born of the Spirit (John 3:5; cf. John 1:12). The Holy Spirit is the attending physician, and more, at the birth of every reborn soul. He also seals the believer unto redemption (2 Cor. 1:21–22; Eph. 1:13–14). He gives the assurance of salvation (1 John 5:4–12).

4. The Holy Spirit's work in the Christian.—When one becomes a Christian, the Holy Spirit takes up his abode in that person's life (John 14:17; 1 Cor. 3:16; 6:19; 2 Cor. 6:16; 1 John 2:27). The New Testament knows nothing of the so-called second blessing. The Holy Spirit is active in the Christian in sanctification. Paul spoke of "being sanctified by the

Holy Ghost" (Rom. 15:16). To sanctify means to make holy, to dedicate to God's service. Sanctification is the gradual process by which this is accomplished. It is growth in the Christian life through Bible study, prayer, and Christian endeavor.

The Holy Spirit is also active in consolation and intercession. He is the comforter (John 14:16, 26). The Greek word for comforter is *paraclete* (Latin-English equivalent, advocate). It is used of "one who stands alongside" as a lawyer, particularly for the defense. He is not only the comforter, the one called alongside in sorrow, but also the one calling alongside, or *challenger;* and God's intercessor in our hearts. Jesus is also called advocate (1 John 2:1) or paraclete. He is the Christian's advocate with God, pleading his case before God; the Holy Spirit is God's advocate, pleading his case before our hearts. Thus God leads us to confession of sin whereby "Jesus Christ the righteous" (1 John 2:1) may hold intercession for us before him for our forgiveness.

Through the Holy Spirit the Christian experiences exhilaration. Paul said, "And be not drunk with wine, wherein is excess; but be filled with the Spirit" (Eph. 5:18). Here he spoke of buoyancy in the Christian's life. Alcoholic beverages tend to give vivacity for a brief period, if not used excessively. Paul said rather for Christians to be filled with the Holy Spirit, who gives a permanent glow to hearts and lives. The most radiant personalities are those whose lives are filled with the presence of God. In like manner, the Holy Spirit is the source of dynamic power. Jesus told his disciples to wait for the power of the Holy Spirit to come upon them before launching out for him (Luke 24:49; Acts 1:8). When he came, it was with symbols of power—wind and fire (Acts 2: 2–3). The early Christians prayed for boldness in persecution, and "the place was shaken . . . and they were all filled with the Holy Ghost [Spirit], and they spake the word of God with boldness" (Acts 4:31). Apart from the Holy Spirit's power all efforts for Christ are in vain. "Not by might, nor by power, but by my spirit, saith the Lord of hosts" (Zech. 4:6).

At this point let us note the fruits of the Spirit. Working in the Christian's life, the Holy Spirit produces the fruits of "love, joy, peace, longsuffering, gentleness, goodness, faith, meekness, temperance" (Gal. 5:22–23). J. Clyde Turner (pp. 100–101) likens these to "three clusters of fruit." First, there is the fruit of the inner life—love, joy, and peace. This love is not sentiment but a governing principle of life. Joy is more than outward pleasure; it is an inner condition not dependent upon environment or circumstances. The peace of God defies understanding. It is an inner calm which enables us to ride the waves of adversity, knowing whose we are and whom we serve. Second, there is the fruit of the outward life —long-suffering, gentleness (kindness), and goodness. Long-suffering (patience) is the ability to bear ill-treatment without revenge, to be composed when dealing with irritating people, and to be calm in the face of abuse or slander. Gentleness is the active side of long-suffering. While the latter is passive, not returning evil for evil, the former is actively engaged in helping others, even those who would do harm. Goodness refers both to purity of life and to unselfish service. While gentleness lends aid when opportunity presents itself, goodness seeks such opportunity. Third, there is the fruit of one's own life—faith (faithfulness), meekness, and temperance (self-control). Faith means loyalty to men and God. Meekness is not weakness; it is strength in the inner self. Temperance is self-control. Only in the Holy Spirit can man master the appetites and passions of his fleshly nature.

In closing this study it is well to recall the various attitudes

Christians may have with regard to the Holy Spirit (Turner, pp. 102 ff.) . We may resist the Spirit (Acts 7:51) by refusing to accept Jesus as Saviour or refusing to acknowledge him as Lord. We may insult the Spirit (Heb. 10:29) by refusing to recognize his place in our lives. We may grieve the Spirit (Eph. 4:30) by failing to obey him. We may quench the Spirit (1 Thess. 5:19) by pouring the water of indifference upon the fire of his zeal in our lives. We may be filled with the Spirit (Eph. 5:18) . All Christians have the Holy Spirit (Rom. 8:9) ; he comes into our hearts with regenerating power. In order to be filled with the Spirit (Acts 6:13) one must be emptied of sin and self and surrendered to the will of God.

In Luke 24:49 Jesus said, "Tarry . . . until ye be endued with power from on high." In the Greek "endued" is a verb form meaning to do something to oneself. We are not to wait passively for God to clothe or fill us. We are to strive actively to rid ourselves of those things which would displace the Holy Spirit and to incorporate into our lives by prayer, Bible study, self-discipline, and spiritual activities those elements conducive to his infilling.

6

Sin

---

*If thou doest well, shalt thou not be
accepted? and if thou doest not well, sin
lieth [coucheth] at the door.*

GENESIS 4:7

THE SUBJECT OF SIN is a much debated one.
Some people deny the reality of sin. But to do so is to deceive
themselves (1 John 1:8) and to make a liar of God (1:10).
Others laugh at sin, but the Bible says that "fools make a
mock at sin" (Prov. 14:9). Still others take pride in their sin
(Isa. 3:9; Rom. 1:32). The most dangerous attitude toward
sin is to tone down its awfulness. Psychology calls sin maladjustment; biology labels it a disease; ethics suggests that it
is a moral lapse; philosophy regards it as a stumbling in the
upward progress of the human race. Paul said in Romans that
"all have sinned, and come short of the glory of God" (3:23).
We shall do well to gain a clear understanding of sin, its
consequences, and its remedy; then shall we better contend
against it.

I. The Meaning of Sin

1. The words for sin.—Several Hebrew words are used to refer to sin: *Awon,* meaning crookedness; *ra,* meaning violence; *nabhal,* or fool. But the basic words are *hata* (Hebrew) and *hamartano* (Greek), both meaning to miss the mark. The idea is that of missing a target. The target is the will and character of God. To miss it is to come short of the glory of God (Rom. 3:23).

2. The basic nature of sin.—Sin is referred to as lawlessness (1 John 3:4); iniquity (Ex. 34:7; Acts 1:18; 8:23); wickedness (Gen. 6:5; 39:9; Rom. 1:29; 1 John 5:19); and offense (Hos. 5:15; Rom. 4:25). But it is at its root transgression (Ex. 34:7; Rom. 5:14) or disobedience (Rom. 5:19; Eph. 2:2). Thus the basic elements in sin are God's will and man's transgression of that will. Man measures or weighs sin, but to God all crossing of his will is sin. What man does after he violates the will of God is secondary. Murder and false witness both are included in the Ten Commandments. We call some men murderers and others liars; God calls both sinners. Sin is, basically, rebellion against the sovereign will of God (Luke 19:14). The ground out of which sin comes is selfishness, wherein men place their wills before the will of God. Thus the root sin of all sin is unbelief. The Holy Spirit convicts nonbelievers of sin, not because they are liars, murderers, thieves, or adulterers, but because they believe not on Jesus (John 16:9).

II. The Origin of Sin

1. Theories of the origin of sin (Mullins, pp. 281 ff.).—One theory says that sin is due to man's possessing a material body. If man destroys the body, he rids it of sin. This idea is based on the ancient Greek belief that matter is inherently evil and gave rise to the monastic orders in the medieval period of history. But matter as such is neither good nor evil. The Bible use of the word "flesh" refers not to the physical body but to the fleshly or rebellious mind or will (Rom. 8:6–7). Some of the worst sins are sins of the mind, will, or spirit: jealousy, envy, and strife, along with fornication, idolatry, murder, and drunkenness (Gal. 5:19–21). Jesus' harshest condemnation was against hypocrisy (Matt. 23). Since Christians are commanded to glorify God in their bodies (Rom. 12:1; 1 Cor. 6:20), it is a matter of will as to the use of the body.

Another theory sees sin as due to man's ignorance or incompleteness. But, as we shall see, sin involves knowledge (Gen. 2:17). It is impossible to eradicate sin through growth in knowledge (Rom. 1:21; 1 Cor. 1:19–25). Two modern but vicious plans of salvation are based on these first two false theories—self-denial and self-expression.

Still a third theory regards sin as being due to man's being a free intelligent being with the power of choice. This is the most satisfactory position with regard to the origin of sin. It fits in with what we know about man: He is a personality endowed with the power of choice and a moral sense which enables him to evaluate in making decisions or choices. It fits in with what we know about God: God is a being of fellowship. For that purpose he made man. With nothing less than a free moral being like himself could God have fellowship. This position agrees with the teachings of the Bible: All that we know about the origin of evil is suggested in a few isolated verses and definitely in Genesis 3:1–7.

2. *The author of evil.*— In this regard it is well to consider the reality of angelic beings (Mullins, pp. 276 ff.). Some would insist that belief in angels is merely a carry-over from heathen and primitive beliefs, since such beliefs were held by

all ancient peoples. But universality does not mean a false belief. Nor can we assume that man is the only intelligent being which God created. The Bible clearly teaches the existence of angels as created beings (Psalm 148:2–5). Usually they appear to men in human form (Gen. 18:2; 19:13), but they also appear in other ways (Matt. 1:20; Luke 2:13; 12:8–9; 1 Cor. 6:3). The word "angel" (Hebrew, *malak;* Greek, *angelos*) simply means messenger. Angels are God's messengers to do his work and will (Heb. 1:14). The "Angel of the Covenant" or "Angel of the Lord" is usually identified with God or the Second Person of the Trinity (Gen. 31:13; 32:30; Judg. 2:1–5; 6:11).

The Bible speaks of fallen angels. The angels were created as holy beings. A holy God could create only holy beings. Jude speaks of "angels which kept not their first estate" (6). Peter spoke of "angels that sinned" and were cast down to hell, bound in "chains of darkness, to be reserved unto judgment" (2 Peter 2:4). It would seem, therefore, that pride was the cause of the fall (cf. 1 Tim. 3:6). This arch-demon is called Satan (adversary or accuser) or devil (slanderer). In contempt for paganism the Jews also called him Beelzebub (Matt. 10:25), after the pagan god Baal. He is pictured as the slanderer of God (Gen. 3:1–7) and man (Job 1); he is our enemy (Matt. 13:39), adversary (1 Peter 5:8), hinderer (1 Thess. 2:18), and accuser (Rev. 12:10). He is the leader of a host of demons (Mark 5:9; Eph. 2:2; 6:12) and with them will be cast into the lake of fire (Matt. 25:41). All lost sinners are children of their father the devil (John 8:44).

3. The beginning of sin.—It is well to remember that the occasion of man's sin grew out of the nature of man himself. Had he been an animal governed only by instinct or a machine operated only by irrevocable law, there would have been no possibility for sin. But since man was endowed with the ability to choose for himself, the possibility for right choices could exist only with the possibility of wrong choices. Although the capacity to sin was an element in his freedom, it did not presuppose the necessity for his sin. Actually, therefore, the key to the problem was the dignity of man. It was in this light that Satan made his first approach to man. His goal was not merely to seduce man but through him to strike his most damaging blow to God, whose will Satan had defied and for which act he had fallen.

The story of the fall is told in Genesis 3:1-7. Note that Satan disguised his true identity. "Now the *serpent* was more subtil than any beast of the field" (3:1; author's italics). While Satan appears before God as Satan (Job 1; Matt. 4), he never does so with man. Paul said that "Satan himself is transformed into an angel of light" (2 Cor. 11:14). To Eve he probably appeared as a graceful, brightly colored flying serpent. Note the curse placed upon him (Gen. 3:14).

In Satan's tempting of Eve, he implied doubt as to God's goodness and love (cf. Matt. 4:3). "Yea, hath God said, Ye shall not eat of every tree of the garden? . . . For God doth know that in the day ye shall eat thereof, then your eyes shall be opened, and ye shall be as gods [God, Elohim], knowing good and evil" (Gen. 3:1-5). Thus Satan not only suggested that God was trying to hold out on Adam and Eve, but he also appealed to Eve's pride and ambition. Furthermore, he sowed doubt as to the sincerity and truth of the word of God (cf. Matt. 4:6). "Ye shall not surely die" (Gen. 3:4). When Eve remonstrated that God's prohibition was for their own good, Satan implied that God had lied (cf. John 8:44). Satan has not changed. He still tells man that the wages of sin is not death but a fuller realization of life.

Again, Satan appealed to the natural desires of the flesh (cf. Matt. 4:8-9). "And when the woman saw that the tree was good for food, and that it was pleasant to the eyes, and a tree to be desired to make one wise, she took of the fruit thereof, and did eat" (Gen. 3:6; cf. 1 John 2:16). W. Hersey Davis defined sin as "an illegitimate expression of a legitimate desire." All the faculties of man are God-bestowed and are therefore good. Satan's business is to entice us to express them in a manner not intended by God (for example, thrift, sex, ambition, acquisitiveness, appetite, intellect, and even faith). Satan reached man through woman. Eve "did eat, and gave also unto her husband with her; and he did eat" (Gen. 3:6). Eve knew of God's command through Adam or by hearsay. Had Eve alone sinned, she would have died, but not the race. As the federal head of the race, in Adam's sin all men died (1 Cor. 15:22). Adam's sin was deliberate.

4. The result of sin.—It is well to note the origin of the universally popular game of "passing the buck" (Gen. 3:12–13). We still seek to alibi for our sin, even to blaming it upon God (Gen. 3:12) or others (Gen. 3:13), but God accepts no such excuses. Instead, God passes sentence upon all involved in sin. To the serpent he said, "Because thou hast done this, thou art cursed . . . ; upon thy belly shalt thou go, and dust shalt thou eat all the days of thy life" (Gen. 3:14). Note Genesis 3:15: no wonder we crush the head of the snake! But the final judgment upon Satan is yet to come (Rev. 20:10).

To Eve God said, "I will greatly multiply thy sorrow and thy conception; in sorrow thou shalt bring forth children; and thy desire shall be to thy husband, and he shall rule over thee" (Gen. 3:16). Note the pain of childbearing. Without sin Eve would doubtless have borne children without pain. She was also to have a subservient position.

But to Adam God said, "Thou shalt not eat of it [the tree of life]: cursed is the ground for thy sake; in sorrow shalt thou eat of it all the days of thy life; thorns also and thistles shall it bring forth to thee; . . . in the sweat of thy face shalt thou eat bread, till thou return unto the ground; . . . for dust thou art, and unto dust shalt thou return" (Gen. 3:17–19). Adam was placed under the sentence of death. It was not pronounced directly upon Eve. Adam was the head of the race, and through him sin and death were bequeathed to all men (1 Cor. 15:22). There is also the hostility of nature because of evil. Thorns and thistles grow spontaneously; herbs must be cultivated. Also in his fallen state man is "of the earth, earthy" (1 Cor. 15:47).

Upon man and woman God pronounced the sentence of spiritual separation from God. "So he drove out the man; and he placed at the east of the garden of Eden Cherubims, and a flaming sword which turned every way, to keep the way of the tree of life" (Gen. 3:24).

There is mercy even in justice. In the curse upon man God foreshadowed the Redeemer (3:15) and mercifully provided in death an escape from the bodies which because of sin are corruptible (1 Cor. 15:50–57). Suppose man could not die! But the truth is that man is now mortal and corruptible (1 Cor. 15:50 ff.) and therefore is not fit for the kingdom of God. To be mortal calls for redemption. It is idle speculation to ask how God would have gotten man out of this earth if evil had not brought death. If God had wanted to do so, he had other ways of doing it. There are a number of examples of this truth: Enoch (Gen. 5:24); Elijah (2 Kings 2:11); Jesus (Acts 1:9–10); and Christians living at the Lord's return (1 Thess. 4:17).

III. The Consequences of Sin

1. The universality of sin.—Here we meet the doctrine of the "total depravity" of man. When Paul said, "For all have sinned" (Rom. 3:23) he spoke of all generations and individuals since Adam. The doctrine of the "total depravity" of man does not mean that all are equally vicious in their sins, nor that there is not some good in all men. It simply means that all men are sinners in that they have transgressed the will of God. The most heinous sins in God's sight are not necessarily murder or adultery. They may be sins of the spirit such as hypocrisy (Luke 18:11; Matt. 23:15). Unbelief is mentioned in the Bible as the greatest sin of all (John 3:18–19). James said that if a person breaks one of the Ten Commandments he is guilty as though he had broken all (2:10 ff.). In Romans 1–3 this truth of total depravity is clearly set forth.

In this passage (Rom. 1–3) man's innate knowledge of God is emphasized. "Because that which may be known of God is manifest in [to] them; for God hath shewed it unto them" (1:19). The witness of God and his will is in every man's heart (1:20*a*), this inner voice being substantiated by evidence in nature (1:20*b*). There is enough knowledge of God in these for the so-called heathen to walk in the will of God and so be saved, if he lives up to this knowledge. However, his sinful nature makes that impossible. Therefore, "they are without excuse: because that, when they knew God, they glorified him not as God, . . . but became vain [empty] in their imaginations, and their foolish heart was darkened" (1:20–21).

The manner of this rebellion was threefold: first, "Professing themselves to be wise, they became fools" (1:22). Their rebellion was in the mind, not the heart. The heart still hungered for God, but their unyielding minds set about to substitute idols for God (1:23). Man is incurably religious. The inner witness of God we call conscience. But conscience alone is not sufficient. By it God whispers that in a given situation man must do right. Man's moral judgment (his mind) tells man what is right. A rebellious mind makes the wrong decision as to what is right. Second, they "changed the truth of God into a lie" (1:25) . Still man's heart hungers for God, but a warped moral judgment leads man to worship and serve "the creature more [rather] than the Creator" (1:25) . Here we see man's worship of man. Third, "They did not like to retain God in their knowledge [acknowledge God]" (1:28) . Here we find the final fruit of rebellious minds. Intellectual idolatry is the most vicious form of heathenism.

Looking back, we discover a progression in culture: idol worship (early men, such as Egyptians, Canaanites, Babylonians, and ignorant savages, yesterday and today) ; worship of man (Greek and Roman gods and goddesses, and Roman emperor worship) , which can be applied to many ancient people as well as to modern people who worship men both dead and living; intellectual sophistication (advanced Greek religion centered in philosophy) , which finds its modern expression in Buddhism, Hinduism, Mohammedanism, and even in the modern deification of intellect.

In each instance notice the threefold clap of doom: "God gave them up" (1:24, 26, 28) . Note that in every case the result was immoral living of the worst sort (1:24, 26–32) . Whenever men, ancient or modern, reject God, the result is always the same. It is well to remember also that these sins are not only of knowledge but of will-power: "Who knowing the judgment of God, that they which commit such things are worthy of death, not only do the same, but have pleasure in them [consent with them] that do them" (1:32) .

This suggests that all men are equally guilty before God. "Therefore thou art inexcusable [without excuse], O man, *whosoever thou art*" (2:1; author's italics) . Paul then proceeded to point out that both Jews (God-worshipers) and Gentiles (heathen) were equally guilty: the Gentile is lost because "as many as have sinned without law [God's revealed Law through Moses] shall also perish without law" (2:12). The Gentile has the law of God in his heart—"Their conscience also bearing witness" (2:15). But their reprobate minds (or perverted moral judgment) had led them astray (2:15). There is, therefore, no hope for the heathen apart from Christ (2:16). The idea that the heathen is not lost unless he hears about Jesus has no foundation in the Scripture. He is lost because he does not live up to the witness of God in his heart; he can be saved only through faith in Christ.

The Jew is lost because "as many as have sinned in the law shall be judged by the law" (2:12). Paul pointed out that the Jew did not live up to the Law (2:17–23) and was therefore under the same condemnation as the heathen (2:25–29). As the teacher of the oracles of God, the Jew's sin even dishonors God among the heathen (2:24). One does not become a Jew because of outward circumcision, the symbol of the Abrahamic covenant, but through inward change or circumcision of the heart (2:28–29). The import of this passage is that the man who has God's law or gospel but rejects it shall receive greater condemnation than the heathen; but "all [Jew and heathen] have sinned, and come short of the glory of God" (3:23).

In Romans 3 a frightful summary pictures all men as they appear in the sight of God. Quoting from the Psalms, Paul drives home his arguments as God speaks, first as a philosopher: "There is none righteous, no, not one: there is none that understandeth, there is none that seeketh after God. They are all gone out of the way, they are together become unprofitable [garbage]: there is none that doeth good, no, not one" (3:10–12; cf. Psalms 14:1–3; 53:1–3). Then God speaks as a physician: "Their throat is an open sepulchre; with their tongues they have used deceit; the poison of asps is under their lips: whose mouth is full of cursing and bitterness" (3:13–14; cf. Psalms 5:9; 10:7; 104:3). Finally, God speaks as a historian: "Their feet are swift to shed blood: destruction and misery are in their ways: and the way of peace have they not known: there is no fear of God before their eyes" (3:15–18; cf. Psalms 10:8 ff.; 36:1). A sordid picture indeed of proud, cultured, sophisticated man—ancient and modern! No wonder the Chinese did not believe the missionary who told him that the New Testament was written two thousand years ago by inspired men. He said that the missionaries wrote it to describe the sins of the modern Chinese people.

2. *The penalty for sin.*—We should realize that as there are degrees of guilt between sins of ignorance or knowledge, sins of impulse or will, so there are degrees of penalty or punishment (Matt. 10:15; 12:31; Luke 12:47–48; John 19:11; Rom. 2:12; cf. Psalm 19:12). It should be remembered that no sin goes unpunished, but the heathen who never heard of Christ shall receive a lesser punishment than the informed man who wilfully rejects Christ. But any degree of hell is horrible beyond human comprehension. Furthermore, men receive a penalty for breaking God's natural, physical, moral, and spiritual laws even in this life. But our concern now is with the penalty for sin, "The wages of sin is death" (Rom. 6:23; cf. Gen. 2:17; 3:22–24).

The first penalty for sin is physical death. God created man to live forever. The tree of life was to be his food (Gen. 1:29; 2:16–17); but when man sinned, he became subject to death (Gen. 2:17; 3:3, 23–24; cf. Rom. 5:12). Since that time, except for Enoch and Elijah, all men have been under the shadow of death (Heb. 9:27). A given death may or may not be the direct result of some sin; but all death is the result of the sin experience of man. The soul or spirit of man is immortal. Physical death comes when the soul or spirit is separated from the body (Luke 23:46; Eccl. 12:7).

But the death of which the Bible most abundantly speaks is spiritual death. Spiritual death does not mean annihilation of the soul but its separation from God. "But your iniquities have separated between you and your God" (Isa. 59:2). When sin separates from God, men are said to be lost from him (Matt. 18:11). But the term most generally used for this condition is "death." The Bible teaches that because of his sinful nature man is born dead (Psalm 51:5). For this reason, from his birth man departs from God (Psalm 58:3). When he reaches the age of intellectual understanding of sin, he is made accountable for his sinful nature and deeds. But man is born dead or condemned (John 3:18). However, it is generally agreed among most Bible scholars that those who die in infancy or who are mentally incompetent are saved by the grace of God in Christ. In the case of natural death the body separated from the spirit is ruined as it returns to the dust. Note that it does not cease to exist as dust; it is only ruined as to its co-ordinated composition. In the matter of spiritual death the soul is not destroyed. But separated from the presence of God, its intended habitat, it is ruined in that it is alienated from God and fails to experience its intended destiny—perfect fellowship with God. Even in this life the result is tragic (Eph. 2:1,3); beyond this life it is unspeakable tragedy (2 Thess. 1:8–9).

Thus the Bible speaks of the second death. In Revelation it is stated that the unredeemed shall be cast into "the lake which burneth with fire and brimstone: which is the second death" (21:8). This is the eternal separation of the spirit or soul from God. The soul will continue to exist eternally with no hope of ever being reunited with God. The Bible knows nothing of purgatory or of a second chance after death!

IV. Salvation from Sin

As terrible as sin is, it offers an opportunity both to God and man—to God in extending his grace to man, to man in accepting God's grace unto salvation (Rom. 8:28; Eph. 2:8–10). Jesus Christ was manifested to destroy the works of the devil (1 John 3:8) and to take away man's sin (1 John 3:5). Thus "there is therefore now no condemnation to them which are in Christ Jesus, . . . for the law of the Spirit of life in Christ Jesus hath made me free from the law of sin and death" (Rom. 8:1–2).

7

The Atonement

And Aaron shall make an atonement upon the horns of it [altar] once in a year with the blood of the sin offering of atonements: once in the year shall he make atonement upon it throughout your generations. EXODUS 30:10

For if, when we were enemies, we were reconciled to God by the death of his Son . . . and not only so, but we also joy in God through our Lord Jesus Christ, by whom we have now received the atonement [reconciliation].
ROMANS 5:10–11

THE WORD "ATONEMENT" means just what it says—at-one-ment. The Hebrew word *kaphar,* translated atonement, means to cover (Ex. 29:36–37; 30:10 ff.; the verb form is found seventy-one times in the Old Testament, the noun nine times). Seven times in the Old Testament the verb is translated to reconcile (Lev. 6:30; 16:20; Ezek. 45:20) or to make reconciliation (Lev. 8:15; Ezek. 45:15,17; Dan. 9:24). The English word "atonement" occurs only one time in the New Testament (Rom. 5:11), where it translates the Greek word *katallagē*, which basically means to reconcile. In Romans 5:10–11 the verb form is so translated twice, while its noun form is rendered atonement. Related forms of this verb are translated reconcile (*apokatallassō*, to change thoroughly from, Eph. 2:16; Col. 1:20–21; *katallassō*, to change thoroughly, Rom. 5:10; 1 Cor. 7:11; 2 Cor. 5:18 ff.; *diallassomai*, to be changed throughout, Matt. 5:24). The word *katallagē* (cf. Rom. 5:11) is also translated reconciliation, meaning a thorough change (Rom. 11:15; 2 Cor. 5:18–19).

The basic idea, therefore, in atonement is to make two as one, to reconcile a difference or to remove a separation between two persons. In Matthew 5:24 the persons involved are two Christians. The word may also refer to cleansing the house of God (Ezek. 45:17,20); settling differences between a wife and her husband (2 Cor. 7:11); the purifying of women after childbirth (Lev. 12); the cleansing of lepers (Lev. 14); the cleansing of men and women with running sores (Lev. 15); and many other instances. In the vast majority of instances the point is a reconciliation between God and man (Ex. 29:36–37; Lev. 16; Rom. 5:10–11; 2 Cor. 5:20).

With reference to the atonement in its strictly spiritual sense, the fundamental concept is the relationship between God and man. God created man for his fellowship (Gen. 2:7; 3:8; Psalms 16:11; 43:4; Rom. 5:11), but sin separated them (Isa. 59:2). With man's expulsion from God's presence (Gen. 3:23–24) God's work of atonement, conceived in eternity, became operative in human history. The perfect fellowship which was broken by man's sin must be restored through an at-one-ment of God and man.

The atonement is not only central in the teachings of the Scriptures and fundamental in the experience of the Christian, but it is inclusive of all theological thought.

I. The Theories of the Atonement (Mullins, pp. 306 ff.)

1. Patristic theory.—The theory held by the early Church fathers was to the effect that the death of Christ was a ransom paid by God to Satan for the souls held captive by Satan (cf. Matt. 20:38). Such a theory is revolting to the teachings of the Bible and to our moral consciousness. It implies that Satan has the souls of men by right of conquest and that God was helpless to deliver them except by paying the ransom that was demanded by Satan. This theory has long since been discarded.

2. Anselm's theory.—This theory dates from the eleventh century and is basic in Roman Catholic theology. It holds to the idea that man's sin violated God's honor and deserves infinite punishment. Since man is morally bankrupt, he cannot pay the debt. Therefore, since Christ was sinless, by his death he accumulated an excess of merit which he placed to the credit of sinners. While this idea is an improvement over the patristic theory, it overlooks the broader teaching of the Bible and emphasizes God's honor and justice while overlooking his infinite love. Likewise it makes the atonement external and mechanical rather than inner and vital.

3. Grotius' theory.—Coming from Hugo Grotius in the seventeenth century, this theory emphasizes God's government. Sin violated God's rule. If he ignored it, God would be endangering his moral governmental principle. In Christ's death God showed the penal principle in divine government as Christ was substituted for man's sin. Thus God could forgive sin without peril to his righteous rule. Here again there is partial truth, but a secondary one which ignores the basic element of God's infinite love which he would reproduce in man.

4. Socinian theory.—Stemming from Faustus Socinus in the sixteenth century and held by modern Unitarians, this theory simply makes Christ's death the death of a martyr to truth which should inspire others toward moral struggle and victory. This idea calls man's sense of guilt and condemnation purely subjective; there is no obstacle to God's pardon other than his lack of repentance. This theory, likewise, is only a partial rendering of the teaching of Scripture. It ignores not only Christian experience but the power of the gospel to transform men.

5. Moral influence theory.—Akin to the preceding one, this theory is held by many modern preachers and theologians. According to this theory there is nothing in the divine nature to be satisfied. Christ's death was to influence men to repent. This theory ignores God's justice and only magnifies his love. It too is only a partial picture.

All of these theories are the result of building a system of thought about one biblical truth while ignoring all others. For instance, the patristic theory emphasizes Satan's role in man's sin experience exclusive of God's nature. Anselm and Grotius magnify God's honor and justice while minimizing his truth and love. Socinus and the moral influence group magnify God's love while forgetting his holiness. We can arrive at the full meaning of the atonement only by considering all of these and more.

II. The Hebrew Day of Atonement

1. The daily and seasonal ministry.—In the tabernacle and later in the Temple God prescribed the daily and seasonal ministry. "Day by day" (Num. 28:3) the priests offered sacrifices for the ceremonial cleansing of the people to fit them for

God's service and fellowship. At certain religious seasons—the sabbath day (28:9), new year (28:11), Passover (28:16), Day of First Fruits (28:26), and Feast of Trumpets (29:1) —sacrifices were made.

2. *The annual ministry.*—But the principal sacrifice, on the Day of Atonement (Yom Kippur), was an annual ministry (Ex. 30:10). Note the time of this annual ministry. It was performed on the tenth day of the seventh month (Lev. 16:29) by the high priest alone for the forgiveness of the sin of all people. The tabernacle was divided into the holy place and the holy of holies. The former was the outer part of the tabernacle in which Aaron and other priests ministered daily. Only on the Day of Atonement could Aaron alone enter into the holy of holies behind the veil. In that place God met him annually in forgiveness for all the sins of the people. Here God was supposed to dwell as symbolized by the pot of manna (Ex. 16), the ark of the covenant containing Aaron's rod which budded (Num. 17:10), and the two tables of law (Ex. 24:12; 25:16). Over the ark lay the mercy seat, a slab of pure gold which was the meeting place between God and Moses (Ex. 25:22). Hovering above the mercy seat were the Cherubim, suggesting the presence of God as accessible in mercy.

3. *The sacrifice.*—The procedure of the high priest on the Day of Atonement (Lev. 16) was prescribed. Five animals were used in the ceremony: "A young bullock for a sin offering, and a ram for a burnt offering" for Aaron (Lev. 16:3; cf. vv. 6, 24); and "two kids of the goats for a sin offering, and one ram for a burnt offering" (Lev. 16:5; cf. vv. 8–10, 24). Aaron cast lots on the goats, one to be for the Lord and the other to be a scapegoat for the people (vv. 7 ff.). Note that verses 3–10 give instructions; verses 11 and following tell of the actual ceremony.

After selecting these animals, Aaron washed himself and

put on the holy linen garments (v. 4). He then offered the bullock as a sin offering for himself and his family (vv. 6, 11). Then, taking a censer, he entered the holy of holies that the incense might cover the mercy seat so that he might not die when he came into the presence of the Lord (v.13). Taking the blood of the bullock, he sprinkled it once on the mercy seat and seven times before it (v.14). Killing the goat, he repeated this ceremony with its blood (v.15). He then sprinkled the horns of the altar with the blood of both (vv. 18–19). Going forth from the tabernacle, he placed his hands upon the scapegoat, confessing over it the sins of the people. This goat, in turn, was led into the wilderness to die (vv. 20–22). Returning to the tabernacle, he removed the linen garments, washed his body, and put on his clothes (vv. 23–24). He then sacrificed the two rams for his sins and those of the people (vv. 24–25). Coming forth, he announced to the people that the atonement for their sins had been made for another year. This ceremony was to be repeated annually "throughout your generations" (Ex. 30:10).

The author of Hebrews tells us that this was but a "figure [pattern]" (Heb. 9:9) or "shadow of good things to come" (Heb. 10:1). Delitzsch called the Day of Atonement "the Good Friday of the Old Testament."

III. The Atonement Through Jesus Christ

1. The motivating element.—The basic element in the atonement is the love of God (John 3:16). Other attributes of God, such as holiness and justice, were violated by man's sin; but basically sin destroyed the fellowship between God and man. Thus God's love was violated. The Old Testament abundantly reveals the broken heart of God (cf. Hosea). In the New Testament the fact of God's love is more clearly revealed. In 1 John he is revealed as love (4:8,16); he is the source of love (4:10). But for his love to be complete required someone to be the object of his love who could, in turn, return it. Sin, therefore, broke the fellowship of love between God and man.

We must remember, however, that God's love is a righteous love. The love relation between God and man could exist only in righteousness. God could not ignore man's sin and continue to be righteous love.

2. *The divine problem.*—How, then, could this breach in fellowship be bridged? Man, though hungry for fellowship with God, was unable to heal the breach (cf. Rom. 1–3). The issue then was up to God. To him the problem was how to remain just [righteous] and yet be the justifier [the One giving righteousness] (Rom. 3:26). Since "the wages of sin is death" (Rom. 6:23), only by death could the breach be healed. The one dying must be sinless (cf. God's rejection of Moses' request in Ex. 32:32; lambs without spot or blemish, Num. 28:3; 1 Peter 1:19). It remained for God to pay the price—hence the incarnation of God in Jesus (John 1:14, 29; Heb. 9:14).

3. *The dual nature of Christ's atoning work.*—The atonement involves both priest and sacrifice. Jesus Christ is both. As priest he is unique and apart. The Old Testament priesthood was of the tribe of Levi; Jesus was of the tribe of Judah (Heb. 7:14). In every sense his priesthood is greater than that of Aaron (Heb. 6:20 to 8:13). Aaron was appointed a priest; Jesus was a priest forever, without beginning of days or end of years (Heb. 6:20 to 7:3). Aaron had successors in his office; Jesus has an abiding priesthood (Heb. 7:11–24). Aaron made sacrifices continually, Jesus once for all (Heb. 7:26–28). Jesus administered a better covenant than Aaron (Heb. 8) and made a superior sacrifice in a better sanctuary (Heb. 9–10).

As sacrifice Jesus is also unique and apart. Aaron ministered in an earthly tabernacle with "meats and drinks, and divers washings, and carnal ordinances [rites or ceremonies]. . . . But Christ being come an high priest . . . by a greater and more perfect tabernacle . . . neither by the blood of goats and calves, but by his own blood he entered in once [*ephapax*, once for all time. *Hapax* means "once for all." With the prefix *ep* the word is made even more emphatic] into the holy place, having obtained eternal redemption for us" (Heb. 9:10–12).

IV. The Effecting of the Atonement

Under the old Covenant or Testament there were annual days of atonement; under the New Covenant there is but one. In his life, death, resurrection, and continuing ministry in heaven Jesus Christ fulfilled (gave full meaning to) every ministry of the tabernacle or Temple both on the Day of Atonement and beyond.

1. The tabernacle itself.— (1) The tabernacle was symbolic of God's presence with his people (Ex. 25:8). Jesus was Emmanuel, God with us (Matt. 1:22–23). He was God become "flesh, and dwelt [tabernacled] among us" (John 1:14). (2) The tabernacle was divided into two parts: the holy place or tabernacle of the congregation, and the most holy place or holy of holies. In the first, man through the priest might approach God daily for the cleansing of his day-by-day sins; in the second, man through the high priest could come only once each year for atonement for sin. Between the two places was a heavy veil suggesting the inapproachable nature of God because of man's sin (Heb. 9:6–8).

In a very real sense Jesus in his life typified the tabernacle of the congregation. Therein were the shewbread, suggestive of Jesus as living Bread (John 6:31–35); the lighted candlesticks, suggestive of Jesus as the Light of the world (John 8:12); and the altar of incense, suggesting Jesus' prayers for us (John 17). The altar of sacrifice would correspond to Calvary. Furthermore, Jesus Christ in his death fulfilled the holy of holies. This we shall see as we delineate the comparison between the Day of Atonement and Jesus' redemptive ministry.

2. *The high priests of the atonement.*—Aaron was one among the people, but in his washing and holy linen garments and the sacrifice of the bullock he was symbolically free from sin (Heb. 9:7). Jesus in his virgin birth was born sinless, yet became one with man in that he was subjected to the limitations of man. He was tempted in all things as we are, yet he was without sin (Heb. 2:18; 4:14–15). But whereas Aaron and his successors were required to minister annually (Lev. 16:32–34; Heb. 9:9), Jesus ministered once for all with no need for repetition (Heb. 9:11–14; 10:10–14).

3. *The sacrifice of the atonement.*—Jesus was also the sacrifice of the atonement. He was the goat upon which the lot of God fell as God was in Christ reconciling the world unto himself (2 Cor. 5:19). Note that the goat had known no sin, yet it was made to become sin for the people. Christ was also "the Lamb of God, which taketh away the sin of the world" (John 1:29). As the goat was slain on the altar, so was Christ slain on the cross (Acts 2:23; 3:15; 4:10). As Aaron entered the holy of holies with the censer (symbolic of prayer), so did Jesus pray on the cross as he entered his holy of holies. Aaron carried the blood of goats and calves annually into the holy of holies; Jesus carried his own blood once for all into the presence of God (Heb. 9:12, 24–28).

4. *The scapegoat of the atonement.*—In his burial Jesus fulfilled the ideal of the scapegoat, which bore the sins of the people away into the wilderness.

5. *The high priest "come forth"* (*Lev. 16:24*) .—After the scapegoat was sent away bearing the sins of the people, Aaron re-entered the tabernacle to come forth dressed in his usual garments, whereupon he sacrificed the rams as burnt offerings (justification) for himself and the people (Lev. 16:24) . Three days after his burial Jesus came forth from the tomb in a glorified body, bearing the evidence of the atonement (Luke 24:39–40; John 20:25 ff.) , yet recognizable to his disciples (Luke 24:31; John 20:16, 20, 28) , as God's vindication or justification of Jesus' deity (Matt. 12:40; Rom. 1:4) and for our justification or salvation (Rom. 4:25; 1 Cor. 15:17–20) .

6. *The proclamation of the atonement.*—It was customary for the high priest to announce to the people at the close of the ceremony that atonement had been made for another year. In turn the people went abroad to proclaim the fact. After Jesus' resurrection he interpreted to his disciples the meaning of his atoning work (Luke 24:25 ff.; cf. John 19:30) and gave his commission that they should proclaim it throughout the earth until the end of time (Matt. 28:19–20; Luke 24:46 ff.; John 20:21) .

7. *The continuing priestly ministry.*—In addition to the sacrifices on the Day of Atonement, the priests daily ministered in the tabernacle for the day-by-day forgiveness of sins. Jesus ascended to the right hand of God "expecting till his enemies be made his footstool" (Heb. 10:12–13) . There he "ever liveth to make intercession for" us (Heb. 7:25; 1 John 2:1) for the continuous forgiveness of sins.

V. The Results of the Atonement

1. *The power of sin.*—The power of sin has been broken. Christ, who knew no sin, suffered the full penalty for our sins (2 Cor. 5:21) as he became our substitute (Isa. 53:1–12) .

He became the end of the law for righteousness on our behalf (Rom. 10:4–10).

2. *God's forgiveness.*—The forgiveness of God is bestowed
upon those who believe in Jesus Christ for salvation. "There
is therefore now no condemnation to them which are in
Christ Jesus. . . . For the law of the Spirit of life in Christ
Jesus hath made me free from the law of sin and death"
(Rom. 8:1–2).

3. *Fellowship.*—The fellowship between God and man has
been restored. When Jesus died on the cross, the veil of the
Temple was torn in two from top to bottom (Matt. 27:51),
enabling us to "come boldly unto the throne of grace, that we
may obtain mercy, and find grace to help in time of need"
(Heb. 4:16). In faith we who were alienated "from the com-
monwealth of Israel, . . . having no hope, and without God
in the world: but now in Christ Jesus ye who sometimes were
far off are made nigh by the blood of Christ. For he is our
peace, who hath made both one [Jew and Gentile] . . .
that he might reconcile [atonement] both unto God in one
body by the cross" (Eph. 2:12–16). In the atonement Jesus
not only restored fellowship between God and man, but between man and man.

Our fellowship with God is that of Father and sons: "But
as many as received him, to them gave he power to become
the sons of God, even to them that believe on his name"
(John 1:12). "For ye have not received the spirit of bondage
again to fear; but ye have received the Spirit of adoption,
whereby we cry, Abba, Father. The Spirit itself beareth
witness with our spirit, that we are the children of God: and
if children, then heirs; heirs of God, and joint-heirs with
Christ" (Rom. 8:15–17).

4. *Final redemption.*—The final redemption is promised.
"So Christ was once offered to bear the sins of many [who be-

lieve on him]; and unto them that look for him shall he appear the second time without sin [apart from sin] unto salvation" (Heb. 9:28) . For this reason we must be busy about the task of proclaiming the atoning death of Christ.

8

Election

Even so then at this present time also there is a remnant according to the election of grace. And if by grace, then is it no more of works. . . . What then? Israel hath not obtained that which he seeketh for; but the election hath obtained it, and the rest were blinded [hardened]. ROMANS 11:5–7

Wherefore the rather, brethren, give diligence to make your calling and election sure. 2 PETER 1:10

THE DOCTRINE OF ELECTION is one of the most vital in the Bible—and one of the least understood. The word "election" does not appear in the Old Testament; it is found in only six verses in the New Testament (Rom. 9:11; 11:5, 7, 28; 1 Thess. 1:4; 2 Peter 1:10). But the word "elect" (Hebrew *bachir*; Greek *eklektos*) appears four times in the Old Testament (Isa. 42:1; 45:4; 65:9, 22) and sixteen times

89

in the New Testament (Matt. 24:22, 24, 31; Mark 13:20, 22, 27; Luke 18:7; Rom. 8:33; Col. 3:12; 1 Tim. 5:21; 2 Tim. 2:10; Titus 1:1; 1 Peter 1:2; 2:6; 2 John 1, 13). *Eklektos* is translated "chosen" seven times in the New Testament (Matt. 20:16; 22:14; Luke 22:35; Rom. 16:13; 1 Peter 2:4, 9; Rev. 17:14). The phrase "elected together with" (*suneklektos*) occurs in 1 Peter 5:13. The root Greek word for election means a choice or a laying out.

Handley Dunelm, in *The International Standard Bible Encyclopedia* (II, 925) says that election "appears to denote an act of Divine selection taking effect upon human objects so as to bring them into special and saving relations with God."

While election involves both God and man, the initiative in election is with God, not with man (John 6:44). In creation the initiative was with God: "In the beginning God created" (Gen. 1:1). Likewise, in redemption the moving force was God: "In the beginning was the Word" (John 1:1).

I. Some Errors Regarding the Doctrine of Election

1. God's will.—One error is that election depends merely upon God's will or good pleasure. The fallacy of this position is that it magnifies some aspects of God's nature to the neglect of all others. It emphasizes God's will and power and minimizes his righteousness and love. Likewise, it ignores the human will and power of choice.

2. Salvation of the few.—Another error is that God wishes to save as few as possible rather than as many as possible. This is in direct contrast to the idea that "God so loved the *world*" (John 3:16; author's italics). The whole tenor of the Bible is that God loves all men equally and endeavors to save them equally.

3. Election of individuals.—A third error is that election relates to certain individuals, with some destined to salvation and others to damnation. This view says that God exhibits his love in the former, while in the latter he demonstrates his justice. Thus the atonement of Christ was not for the whole world but for the elect alone. This, however, is a direct negation of the comprehensive teachings of Scripture (John 3:16; Rev. 22:17). There are two schools of theology on this point: Calvinism believes that Christ died to save some, the elect; Arminianism believes that he died to save all men.

4. Fatalism.—A final error is that election tends toward fatalism. Such a view says that some will be saved and others lost, regardless of what they do. Therefore, evangelism is unnecessary. In like manner are all events of man's life explained. This reasoning makes God the perpetrator of evil. It makes man a puppet on a string. Election never appears in the Scriptures as mechanical or blind destiny. It has to do with a God who is love and with a man who is morally responsible (1 John 4:8–10; Acts 2:37–41; Rom. 10:13). Election never appears as a violation of human will (Matt. 23:37–38).

II. The Twofold Elements Basic in Election

1. The sovereignty of God.—There are two ways to regard this truth—abstract and concrete (Mullins). The sovereignty of God, considered in the abstract, simply means that God, being all-powerful, can do as he pleases apart from any other consideration, such as the rights or well-being of others or all the attributes of his nature. An example of this may be seen in Matthew 20:1–16. Here each laborer received the same wages regardless of the hours worked simply because the owner wished it so. However, there is much more in this parable than that one idea, e.g., justice (vv. 13–14) and mercy (vv. 14 ff.).

But if the sovereignty of God is considered in the concrete, all of God's sovereign dealings as related in the Scriptures must be included. Here, in the words of Mullins (p. 267), we discover that God "keeps the reigns of government in his hands. He guides the universe to his own glorious end. That end embodies the highest ideals of holiness and love" (Isa. 54:8; 55:1–9; Jer. 31:3; Eph. 3:1–11).

2. *The free will of man.*—Over against the sovereignty of God the Bible places the free will of man. God made man in his own image (Gen..1:27). Man is a personality with the power of choice (Gen. 3:1–6); he is capable of a sense of guilt (Gen. 3:7); he is morally responsible for his decisions (Gen. 3:8–24; Jer. 31:29–30; Ezek. 18:2; Rom. 1–3).

3. *The impossibility of harmonizing these two facts.*— On the level of finite intellect the sovereignty of God and the free will of man cannot be harmonized, but in the infinite wisdom of God there is no conflict (Isa. 54:8–9; Rom. 11:33 ff.). But even human reason can help us to understand, in part, this mystery. We know that divine sovereignty must not cancel human freedom, else man becomes a mere machine incapable of fellowship with God. Furthermore, this would make God responsible for man's sinful acts.

However, if we remember that God is a God of law, the mystery is partially explained. The presence of law in the physical, moral, and spiritual realms hardly needs to be proved. Science has demonstrated the role of law in nature (Gen. 1:24–25; 8:22). By it health is preserved and the ground is tilled; natural law makes possible orderly living on the earth. Daily observation demonstrates that in the moral and spiritual realms the wages of sin is death (Rom. 6:23). It is well to remember that all of God's laws are beneficent. Only when we violate them do we pay the penalty in suffering and death. The evil in nature and in man is not by the express will but by the permissive will of God.

However, we must also remember that the very nature of God's dealings with us through law constitutes a self-limitation upon God. Thus he does not act merely by capricious will but by the laws which he has established. The final answer to all things, therefore, is in the will of man. If his life corresponds to God's laws, well and good. But if his will runs counter to these laws, the wages of sin is death in whatever realm it may be. Obedience or disobedience to God's laws determines the outcome.

But even so, God has higher laws than those known to man by which God overrules man's rebellious will. By the knowledge of these higher laws (Gen. 1:28) man is able to live a fuller life and to overrule his own errors. But even beyond man's knowledge God works by his laws in the realm of the miraculous.

It is in this final thought that we find understanding of the dealings of God with man in salvation. When man sins, God imposes the higher law of his mercy and grace (Eph. 2:1–10). God takes the initiative to save miraculously in accord with his righteousness and love. Hence come the incarnation in Jesus and his crucifixion, resurrection, and continuing intercession. But the free will of man is involved, for he must either accept or reject the saving overtures of a righteous and loving God. Even the sovereignty of God is limited by God's moral and spiritual laws and by the nature of the free will of man.

Therefore, the doctrine of election refers to a plan of salvation for all men and not simply to the capricious choice of some men and the rejection of others. God in his sovereignty has elected a plan of salvation for all men. It is a plan based on grace and not merit (cf. Matt. 20:1–16). Those who in their free will accept it are saved; those who reject it are by their own free will lost. "Many [or all] be called [or elected], but few [those who conform to the elected plan] chosen" (Matt. 20:16).

4. The cognate terms relative to the problem.—"For whom he did *foreknow,* he also did *predestinate* to be conformed to the image of his Son. . . . Moreover whom he did predestinate, them he also *called:* and whom he called, them he also *justified:* and whom he justified, them he also *glorified*" (Rom. 8:29–30; author's italics). The foreknowledge of God simply means that God knows all things before they happen. God knew beforehand who would accept or reject his overture of grace.

But a person's foreknowledge of an event does not make it a part of his will or planning. In his finite foreknowledge he may know that automobiles are going to crash and people will be killed. But he does not will or cause it. The infinite foreknowledge of God removes all uncertainty, but it does not make God responsible. He knows who will reject his grace, but he does not will it or cause it. Predestination with regard to salvation, on the other hand, simply means that God has predetermined that those who respond affirmatively to his call or election will be *justified,* or declared righteous, and furthermore will be *glorified.* All of this is "according to his purpose" (Rom. 8:28; Eph. 3:11).

III. The Twofold Operation of Election

We cannot fully understand the doctrine of election unless we see in it God's purpose of salvation for all men. This doctrine is not based upon arbitrary choice but upon the fulfilment of God's "eternal purpose which he purposed in Christ Jesus our Lord" (Eph. 3:11). To accomplish this purpose God elected first a people and second, individuals.

1. The election of people.—God elected individuals and families. First, God chose Noah and his family (Gen. 6:8) to be the channel of his blessings to mankind. Second, he chose Abraham and his seed: "And I will make of thee a great nation, and I will bless thee, and make thy name great; and *thou shalt be a blessing:* and I will bless them that bless thee, and curse him that curseth thee: and in thee shall *all families of the earth* be blessed" (Gen. 12:2–3; author's italics) . Note the condition and the racial blessing. We do not comprehend the election of Abraham unless we see also God's worldwide purpose of grace. The covenant with Abraham was basic in his redemptive purpose.

Of Abraham's two sons, Ishmael and Isaac, God chose or elected Isaac (Gen. 15:4; 17:16; 21:12; Rom. 9:7) ; of Isaac's two sons God chose Jacob (Mal. 1:2–3; Rom. 9:13) ; and from Jacob's loins came the twelve tribes of Israel. Note that "love" and "hate" in Malachi 1:2–3 and Romans 9:13 contain the element of choice. God had to choose one or the other; therefore, he loved or chose Jacob and hated or rejected Esau. All the above choices were sovereign, but this sovereignty was based upon God's foreknowledge that those chosen possessed characteristics which would make them suited to God's purpose. Even so, their response was one of free will. Note instances where they acted otherwise (Gen. 9:21; 12:11 ff.; 25:25 ff.; 26:7 ff.; 27:1–46) .

The crux of this matter is seen in the election of the nation, Israel. When God was ready to redeem Israel from Egypt, he proposed to carry out through them his covenant with Abraham (Ex. 6:5–8) . Thus he elected a nation. This covenant with Israel was sealed after their deliverance from Egypt. Note that God covenants only with a redeemed people. "Now therefore, *if* ye will obey my voice indeed, and keep my covenant, *then* ye shall be a peculiar treasure unto me above all people: *for all the earth is mine:* and ye shall be unto me a *kingdom of priests,* and *an holy nation*" (Ex.

19:5–6; author's italics). God was sovereign in making this proposal; Israel exercised her free will in accepting it (Ex. 19:8).

Note that this was a conditional covenant. God's sovereign election was still combined with Israel's free will in accepting or rejecting, then and later, the covenant. But this did not mean that God loved Israel more than other nations. She was to be a priest-nation through which God would extend his love to all people. But Israel forgot the responsibility and remembered only the privilege of being a peculiar treasure. The prophetic utterances bristle with challenges for Israel to accept in reality the conditions of the covenant. "It is a light thing that thou shouldest be my servant to raise up the tribes of Jacob, and to restore the preserved [desolations] of Israel: I will also give thee for a light to the Gentiles [heathen], *that thou mayest be my salvation unto the end of the earth*" (Isa. 49:6; author's italics).

When finally it became apparent that Israel would not honor the covenant, God, as sovereign, promised a new covenant (Jer. 31:31 ff.; Heb. 8:8 ff.). The sovereign will of God is grounded in his saving love. He never changes his eternal purpose, though he changes his procedure according to man's free will. Thus we come to the incarnation of God in Jesus Christ, who was not merely a Jew but the Son of man. Here again we see the worldwide redemptive purpose of God. Christ died for all men; his commission included "all nations" (Matt. 28:19–20).

At this point we note the election of a people, the new Israel. According to Matthew 21, God rejected national Israel. The parables of the two sons (vv. 28–32) and the wicked husbandmen (vv. 33–41) clearly relate how repeatedly Israel's free will had rejected God's sovereign will with regard to his covenant. By their own words Jesus condemns the Jews:

"He will miserably destroy those wicked men, and will let out his vineyard [cf. Isa. 5:1–7] unto other husbandmen, which shall render him the fruits in their seasons" (v. 41). Jesus replied: "Therefore say I unto you, The kingdom of God shall be taken from you, and given to a nation bringing forth the fruits thereof. . . . And when the chief priests and Pharisees had heard his parables, they perceived that he spake of them [as representative of the nation]" (vv. 43, 45).

The sequel to these words is found in 1 Peter 2:4–10 with reference to Christian people. Compare this passage with Exodus 19:5–6 and Matthew 21:42–44: note "stone," "corner," "builders rejected," "head of the corner," "broken," "grind him to powder" (Matt.); and "chief corner stone," "elect, precious" (cf. Ex.), "confounded," "disobedient," "stone of stumbling, and a rock of offence" (1 Peter). "But ye are a *chosen generation; a royal priesthood,* an *holy nation,* a *peculiar people;* that ye should shew forth the praises of him who hath called you out of darkness into his marvellous light [cf. Isa. 60:2–3]: which in time past were *not a people,* but are now the people of God [cf. Hos. 1:9]: which had not obtained mercy, but now have obtained mercy" (1 Peter 2:9–10; author's italics).

The similarity between these three passages in Exodus, Matthew, and 1 Peter cannot be accidental. They are an expression of the electing purpose and grace of God. A careful study of Romans will reveal that the promise of God was not to the physical seed of Abraham (Rom. 4; cf. Matt. 3:7–9) but to the spiritual seed. Paul was careful to point out in Romans 9–11 that "they are not all Israel, which are of Israel. . . . They which are the children of the flesh, these are not the children of God: but the children of the promise are counted for the seed" (9:6–8). This entire section (Rom. 9–11) points out that not all members of national Israel are within the promise. Only those, Jews as well as Gentiles, who have accepted Christ are spiritual Israel.

In Ephesians, probably next to the last letter written by Paul, the apostle clearly set forth the truth that the eternal purpose of God is no longer through one nation but through the church, the redeemed through Christ (Eph. 3, note especially vv. 10–11), which is made up of redeemed people of all races and nations. This truth may be summarized by saying that God's sovereign will elects those who are to be his "royal priesthood" and "holy nation" for the salvation of all men. The free will of man either accepts or rejects this relationship to his own loss.

2. The election of individuals.—The difference between God's election of a nation as the means of achieving God's saving purpose and his election of individuals unto salvation is that the former is a matter of God's people's losing their opportunity, while the latter is a matter of a lost person's failing to receive salvation. While an opportunity may be grasped and lost, salvation once received is never lost. But saved people may lose their opportunity to become a part of God's larger redemptive purpose for all other men.

Note, further, God's initiative in his electing grace. Again we repeat that God in his sovereignty has elected a plan of salvation. He has taken the initiative in offering salvation to all men. This is seen in many Scripture passages: John 3:16; 6:37; 6:44; Acts 13:48. Again, in Romans 9–11, there is not only the aforementioned lesson regarding national and spiritual Israel but the matter of the salvation of individual Jews and Gentiles. The sovereign will of God and the free will of man is obvious in both cases (cf. 9:11–13). Election is not a matter of capricious choice on God's part but of his foreknowledge of what man's response will be to his proffered grace.

Man's response is a free choice. God has elected salvation to all who, in freedom of will, will call on him or who will meet the conditions of the elected plan of salvation (cf. Rev. 22:17). In short, God has provided in his election all that is necessary for man's salvation. He has made man a free moral agent; he is a person (Mullins) of knowledge (2 Cor. 5:11); conscience (2 Cor. 5:11); hope (Rom. 8:24); love (1 Cor. 13); sorrow (2 Cor. 7:10); and will (Matt. 23:37; John 5:40; Rev. 22:17), with the power to accept salvation in faith or reject it in unbelief. When Christ cried, "It is finished" (John 19:30), the sovereign God had done all that he could do. Through his church he uses the Bible, music, preaching, and teaching that the Holy Spirit may aid men in making a favorable response. But the response lies in the free will of man. Scripture passages abound to this effect (John 3:16; 5:24; 20:31; Acts 2:41–42; 16:31; Rom. 10:10).

But like Israel as a nation, so we as individuals must remember that salvation is not merely a privilege to be enjoyed but a blessing to be shared (cf. Gen. 12:2). In John 15:16 Jesus said, "Ye have not chosen me, but I have chosen you, and ordained [appointed] you, *that ye should go and bring forth* fruit" (author's italics). Here is election both to salvation and to evangelism. In both the free will of man determines the final result. By free will men can elect to be saved but elect to be barren Christians. God forbid! The Epistle to the Hebrews is a warning against such a life. (See Hobbs, *Studies in Hebrews.*)

3. The hardening of man's heart.—Certain passages seem to teach that God is the active agent in the hardening of men's hearts against his proffered will (Ex. 7:3, 13; 10:1). In a sense the Scriptures often attribute events, whether good or evil, to God (Isa. 45:7). In these passages the sovereignty of God is under consideration. But remembering the free will of man, we must interpret this and other such cases in the light of the permissive will of God. In practically all of these instances cited the context shows that the hardening of the heart was due to the voluntary acts of men themselves and not to God (Ex. 8:15, 32; 9:27–28). The Bible abundantly and clearly declares that men bring upon themselves moral and spiritual blindness by their persistence in sin. God permits his laws to work to the end that by their free choice men lose their moral sense and become spiritually blind (Matt. 13:13 ff.; Mark 4:11–12; Luke 8:10). As Mullins says, "A judicial blindness or hardening came as a result of their own sin. It was the result of God's action only as expressed in the laws of their moral constitution" (p. 357).

In conclusion we quote Mullins' definition of election: "Election is not to be thought of as a bare choice of so many human units by God's action independently of man's free choice and the human means employed. God elects men to respond freely. He elects men to preach persuasively and to witness convincingly. He elects to reach men through their native faculties and through the church, through evangelism and education and missionary endeavor. We must include all these elements in election. Otherwise we split the decree of God into parts and leave out an essential part" (p. 347).

9

Salvation

I have waited for thy salvation, O Lord.   GENESIS 49:18

And thou, child, shalt be called the prophet of the Highest: for thou shalt go before the face of the Lord to prepare his ways; to give knowledge of salvation unto his people by the remission of their sins.
       LUKE 1:76–77

THE WORD "SALVATION" has many meanings in the Bible. It is a noun which comes from the Greek verb which in the Septuagint is used to translate Hebrew words meaning to save, to keep safe and sound, and to rescue from danger or destruction. It is the opposite of *apollumi,* meaning to destroy, from which we get the name Apollyon, one of the names of Satan (Rev. 9:11). In the New Testament it is sometimes used in the sense of saving or rescuing from danger or destruction (Matt. 8:25; 14:30; 24:22; Acts 27:20, 31; 2 Peter 4:18). It is also used to refer to healing (Matt. 9:22), both physical and spiritual (Luke 7:50). By far the greatest use of this verb is to mean deliverance from the messianic judgment (Joel 2:32); to save from evils which obstruct the messianic deliverance (Matt. 1:21; Rom. 5:9; James 5:20); to make one a partaker of the salvation offered by Christ (Matt. 19:25; John 3:17) (Thayer, p. 610).

The noun form in Hebrew carries the general idea of safety or ease (Ex. 14:13; 2 Sam. 22:51), while in the Greek form it denotes safety or soundness (Luke 1:69 ff.). Two different Greek words call for special notice. *Sōtērios* refers to the one bringing salvation (Titus 2:11; cf. Luke 2:30; 3:6; Acts 28:28). *Sōtēria* and *sōtērion,* the more widely used forms, have a variable meaning in keeping with the uses of the root verb *sōzō*. It sometimes means deliverance or preservation from enemies (Acts 7:25), or preservation of physical life, safety (Acts 27:34), or health (Heb. 11:7). It is largely employed to express the idea of salvation in a spiritual sense (Luke 19:9; John 4:22; Rom. 10:10). It is in this sense that we shall deal with it.

I. The Threefold Nature of Salvation

Unfortunately we commonly regard salvation in one sense only, that of redemption from sin. But a careful examination of the use of the word and its equivalents will reveal that salvation in the spiritual sense is used to express three different ideas: instantaneous, continuing, and ultimate.

1. The instantaneous salvation.—This is the idea of redemption from sin (Acts 2:21; 16:31; Rom. 10:10). Carrying the concept of deliverance from the penalty of sin, this experience occurs immediately upon the individual's trusting in Jesus as Saviour. This is a fixed condition expressed in the idea of the perseverance of the saints, meaning that all who are truly saved will endure or persevere to the end. It is synonymous with being born again (John 3:3–7); enrolling in Jesus' school (Matt. 11:29); spiritual marriage (John 3:29); or adoption into the family of God (Rom. 8:15–23).

2. *The continuing salvation.*—This is the figure of growing in grace, knowledge, and service of and for Christ (2 Peter 3:18; Phil. 2:12; Heb.; 2 Cor. 1:6). It is at this point that many err in understanding the relation of works to salvation. While the immediate redemption of the soul from the penalty of sin is by grace through faith (Eph. 2:8–9), God has also ordained that believers should walk in good works for the salvation of their Christian lives (Eph. 2:10; Phil. 2:12–13). When the devil loses our souls to Christ, he seeks to insure that we shall lose our lives to him. Alas, how very often we find that he succeeds! This continuing salvation we call sanctification, whereby we grow into the likeness of Christ our Lord.

3. *The ultimate salvation.*—This reference is to the final culmination of the redemptive process, or the total of the benefits and blessings in heaven, which shall be for all the redeemed in proportion to their faithfulness in Christian service (Rom. 13:11; 1 Thess. 5:9; Heb. 9:28; Rev. 12:10). All Christians shall be saved, but there will be a difference in rewards. This final phase we refer to as glorification, or the full realization of the meaning of salvation. Now let us more closely examine each of these. For convenience we shall con-sider these three phases under two headings: salvation in time and salvation in eternity.

II. Salvation in Time

1. *The instantaneous salvation.*—In previous chapters we have noted the sinfulness of man, the initiative of God in the election of a plan of salvation, the atoning work of Christ, and the work of the Holy Spirit in conviction. Thus we are

brought to a consideration of the elements involved in the immediate redemption of the soul.

Redemption is by grace apart from works (Eph. 2:8–10). Since man is totally sinful (Rom. 3:23), he could be saved only by grace (Rom. 3:24). Grace comes from a Greek word (*charis*), which basically means to make a gift (2 Cor. 8:1–9), to forgive a debt, to forgive a wrong, and finally, to forgive sin. It denotes kindness or favor shown by a master toward his servants, and so of God to man (Luke 1:30). It refers to the merciful act of God whereby he bestows forgiveness of sin upon those who accept it through Christ (John 1:12–14; Eph. 2:8). The idea of grace rules out good works, baptism, or any other man-performed act as the ground of redemption. Because man is a sinful and weak creature, a force greater than himself must provide the way.

Redemption is a progressive experience. While these progressive steps may occur in one fraction of a second, they are all necessary for a genuine spiritual experience. Following conviction there is the element of repentance. Two words for repentance occur in the New Testament. *Metamelomai* expresses the emotional element in repentance. It means regret. It may be of a godly sort leading to genuine repentance (2 Cor. 7:9–10); it may mean sorrow without genuine repentance (Luke 18:23); or it may mean merely regret that one got caught in his sinful deeds (Matt. 27:3). *Metanoia*, on the other hand, means a change of mind or attitude. The idea is more than a mere intellectual change; it involves the will as well as the heart (Mark 1:4, 14–15; Luke 17:3; Acts 2:38; Rom. 2:4). It is intellectual in that it produces a change in the individual's view of God and sin: from hating God he loves him; from loving sin he hates it. This idea involves a change of feeling, not simply with regard to what sin does to man but what it does to God (2 Cor. 7:9–10). It involves a change of will. One gets a new purpose in life as he forsakes sin and turns to God (Acts 9:1–6).

Repentance is followed by the exercise of faith. Repenting, one turns to God in faith as he trusts in Jesus for salvation. Faith involves intellect, for there must be something or someone in which to believe (2 Tim. 1:12). But intellectual belief is not enough. The devils believe and tremble (James 2:19). Faith also involves assent that Christ's death does suffice for sin (Acts 2:36–41). Faith furthermore includes the volitional act of trust. Being convinced of the saving efficacy of Christ, the individual surrenders his soul to him (Rom. 1:16). The New Testament abounds in this truth. Paul, in Romans, declares salvation to be a matter of faith from beginning to end (1:17). The climax of Paul's argument is in chapters 4–5, where he proves that even Abraham was saved not by works but by faith.

Conviction, repentance, and faith result in the experience of conversion. This word, including both repentance and faith, refers to the outward evidence of an inner change. The inner change is repentance and faith; the outward evidence is turning from the old life of rebellion against God to one of service to God (Acts 9:1–22; James 2:14–26; cf. Matt. 3:8; 7:16,20). The word "convert" is also used in the New Testament in the sense of the reconsecration of a Christian (Luke 22:31–32).

The effect of conversion in the unbeliever's heart is the experience of regeneration. This is a change wrought by the Holy Spirit, sometimes called being born again (John 3). It changes men from sons of Satan (John 8:44) into sons of God (John 1:12). In Christ we are new creatures or creations (2 Cor. 5:17). We are said to be begotten of God (1 Peter 1:23). Another figure used to express this idea is that of adoption into the family of God (Rom. 8:14–17). The emphasis here is not on the legal aspect but upon the vital union with God in Christ.

The outcome is the state of justification. This is the judicial act of God whereby he declares the sinner righteous as though he had never sinned, removes the condemnation of sin, and restores him to divine favor (John 3:17–18; 5:24; Rom. 1:17; 8:1–2, 30). The word "justification" translates the Greek word *dikaioō*, which means, not that one is just or righteous, but that he is declared just or righteous. In Romans Paul develops this idea of how a man may be righteous before God. He concludes that justification is not by works but is a matter of faith from beginning to end (1:17; 3:28).

At this point we note a conflict in religious thought. Beginning in the first century some insisted that faith plus works produce justification (Gal. 2:3; cf. Acts 15). The tone of all New Testament teachings is to the effect that men are saved by grace through faith apart from works (Eph. 2:8–10; Gal. 5:1–7). "The just [those declared righteous] shall live by his faith" (Hab. 2:4) is the only verse from the Old Testament quoted three times in the New Testament (Rom. 1:17; Gal. 3:11; Heb. 10:38). One of Paul's favorite expressions is "in Christ." There is no condemnation to those who are "in Christ" (Rom. 8:1). Believers are alive unto God "through [in] Christ" (Rom. 6:11). Those "in Christ" are new creatures or creations (2 Cor. 5:17). We are "created in Christ Jesus unto good works" (Eph. 2:10; see also John 14:20 and 1 John 2:6).

This suggests the idea of perseverance. Can the Christian, once saved, ever be lost again? The thundering answer of Scripture is no. The words eternal or everlasting life negate this idea (John 3:16–18). This life is not a future prospect but a present reality (cf. John 5:24). In Ephesians 2:8 we read, "For by grace have ye been saved" (author's translation). This is a perfect passive tense referring to an action in the past, done to one by another, which still continues and will continue in the future. The term "falling from grace" comes from expressions found in Galatians 5:4 and Hebrews 12:15. The true reading is "fall away from." The idea is that God proposes salvation by grace. To seek salvation by works is to fall away from the way of salvation by grace. When we accept Christ, we become "sons of God" (John 1:12; Rom. 8:15 ff.; cf. Heb. 12:5–11). We may be disobedient sons whom God chastens, but we remain God's children.

2. *The continuing salvation.*—The purpose of God in redemption as far as time is concerned is the production of holy men and women as members of a holy society (Mullins). The first is accomplished in the instantaneous salvation. All the saved are called "saints" in the New Testament (Acts 9:13, 32, 41; 26:10; Rom. 1:7; 1 Cor. 1:2; 2 Cor. 1:1; Heb. 6:10; Jude 3; Rev. 5:8; and others). The second is brought about by the continuing salvation or sanctification.

The idea of sanctification comes from Hebrew (*qadesh*) and Greek (*hagiazō*) words meaning to separate or to set apart for the service of God (Ex. 13:2; 29:43; Num. 7:1; 1 Chron. 23:13; John 10:36; 17:17, 19). Originally the word "holy" (Isa. 6:3) meant anything set apart for the service of a god. As the word came to be associated with God, it took on the moral content of purity.

It is well to note two wrong views of sanctification. First, it does not give ground for loose living. This thought was present in the first century and still persists today. This view takes on two aspects. "Shall we continue in sin, that grace may abound?" (Rom. 6:1). If grace much more abounds where sin abounds, why refrain from sin? In Romans 6–7 Paul clearly points out that such is impossible for the Christian: note the figures of death (6:2–11), slave and master (6:12–

23), man and wife (7:1–25). Again, "Use not liberty for an occasion to the flesh" (Gal. 5:13). In short, do not use liberty as an excuse for license.

Second, sanctification does not refer to perfection. There are those who so take it. Some passages seem to teach this (Matt. 5:48; Eph. 1:4; Phil. 3:15; Heb. 6:1; James 1:4; 1 Peter 1:16), but a careful study reveals otherwise. The word "perfect" is the idea of a goal or an end in view. Anything which performed as it was intended is regarded as perfect, even though it might have imperfections in it, like a knife which cuts even though it has flaws. In that sense, then, we are exhorted to set as our goal perfection so that we shall strive to become as God intends us to be, both in character and service. The Bible quite clearly teaches that so long as we are in the flesh we shall have sin in our bodies (Rom. 7:14–25; James 3:2; 1 John 1:6–10). But this does not justify sinful living. We are repeatedly exhorted to refrain from such that we may become fit instruments for God's service (cf. Rom. 6:12 ff.). We are exhorted to struggle against sin (James 4:7).

The fact that sanctification does not refer primarily to getting rid of sin is seen in Jesus' prayer, "For their sakes I *sanctify* myself, that they also might be sanctified through the truth" (John 17:19; author's italics). Jesus dedicated himself as God's means of salvation that those who are his might also be dedicated to the proclamation of God's redeeming love. This implies that through faith we shall not only be in him for life but also for fruit-bearing. This involves not only trust but holy living as well.

Sanctification has a threefold nature. It is instantaneous in that the moment we trust in Jesus we are dedicated to God and his service (Acts 9:6, 15–16). The Holy Spirit takes up his abode in us (Acts 10:44 ff.; 1 Cor. 6:19), that he might develop and use us (John 14:26; cf. Luke 24:49; Acts 1:8). It is continuous in that we "go on growing in grace, and in the knowledge and service of our Lord and Saviour Jesus Christ" (2 Peter 3:18, author's translation). Thus sanctification is both instant and progressive. It is at this point that good works enter into our Christian experience (Eph. 2:10; cf. Matt. 5:13–16). We are not redeemed by good works, but our Christian lives are sanctified by them. The sin of negligence causes us to lose our lives so far as usefulness in God's service is concerned (Matt. 16:24–27; cf. Heb. 2:1–3). Salvation is ultimate in that those who are genuinely saved will persevere in fruit-bearing (Matt. 3:8; 7:16; John 15:2–16) unto the final perfection and reward which they will receive in heaven (John 4:36–37; cf. Matt. 25:14–46).

3. The two pictures of salvation.—First, note the new birth or sonship. When Paul used the figure of adoption (Rom. 8:14 ff.), he was referring to the same thing of which Jesus spoke when he used the figure of the new birth (John 3:7). The thought is that by the work of the Holy Spirit we become sons of God (John 1:12). The very moment a child is born he is the child of his father. He does not wait until he is full-grown to be born. But at the moment of birth he begins to grow in wisdom, stature, and usefulness. This he continues all his life until death.

So when we are born again, we do not wait until we are full-grown in Christ to become children of God. All that is necessary is that we are born of the Spirit. However, the moment we are born again we are to begin our growth in spiritual knowledge and stature that we may serve God. The extent that we do that determines the quality of Christian life we shall live, but we can never be unborn from being God's children. We may be dwarfed or freakish in God's sight, but we are still his.

Second, note the figure of discipleship. In Matthew 11:29 Jesus said, "Take my yoke . . . and learn of me." The figure of taking the yoke refers to a child's enrolling as the pupil of a teacher. In short, Jesus said, "Become my pupil." Pupil means disciple. A child does not wait until he receives a diploma from college to enrol as a pupil. The emphasis is not on how much the pupil knows but on his willingness to turn himself over to the teacher for instruction. A person, even a child, does not need to know but to trust. In a mystical sense, then, becoming a Christian is trusting Jesus, the Teacher, as we submit ourselves to him. For the rest of our lives we shall be his pupils as he teaches us his will, way, and work. Obviously one may be a poor pupil, but he loses the joy of great knowledge utilized in service and a life well invested for God.

In this light we understand the Great Commission (Matt. 28:19–20). Jesus said, in effect, "As ye go, make disciples [pupils] of all nations, baptizing them, . . . teaching them to observe all things. . . ." The command included three things: make disciples, baptize, teach. How tragic that so many are born but never grow into full stature in Christ Jesus (Eph. 4:13) ! They enrol in his school, but when they should be teaching others, they are still trying to learn the "first principles of the oracles of God" (Heb. 5:12–14) ! For such their souls are saved, but their lives are lost (1 Cor. 3:12–15; cf. Heb. 2:1–3; 3:7–12; 5:12 to 6:9; 10:26. See Hobbs, *Studies in Hebrews,* on these passages) .

It is well at this point to consider briefly the priesthood of all believers. This phrase simply means that all Christians are priests (Rev. 1:5–6). As such we enjoy a direct approach to God (Matt. 27:51; Heb. 4:16) . We need no priest, saint, sacrament, or ordinance by which to come to God for grace or forgiveness (1 Tim. 2:5–6; cf. Heb. 8:6; 9:15; 12:24) . We can pray directly to God in Jesus' name (Matt. 6:5–13;

Luke 18:1) , knowing that the Holy Spirit helps us when we pray (Rom. 8:26) and that we have an "advocate with the Father, Jesus Christ the righteous" (1 John 2:1) . We can also read and interpret God's Word for ourselves (Heb. 8:10–11) in the assurance that the Holy Spirit will illumine our minds for its understanding (John 14:26; cf. Luke 24:32, 45) .

But this priesthood also involves responsibility. "All things are of God, who hath reconciled us to himself by Jesus Christ, and *hath given to us the ministry of reconciliation*" (2 Cor. 5:18; author's italics) . In this relation the Great Commission is our challenge (Matt. 28:19–20) , and Hebrews 12:1 ff. is our example.

III. The Salvation in Eternity

In Jesus' high priestly prayer (John 17) he prayed, "Those that thou gavest me *I have kept*" (v. 12; author's italics; cf. John 6:37–40) . Though men may be faithless, he is faithful. To that end the Scriptures teach the ultimate salvation of all who believe in Jesus (Rom. 13:11; 1 Thess. 5:9; Heb. 9:28; 1 Peter 1:5, 10) . The idea of degrees of reward according to Christian living will be treated later. The thought here is that all who truly trust in Jesus shall be with him in glory. The message of Revelation is the victory of Christ and the believer's victory in him: "Now is come salvation . . for the accuser [Satan] of our brethren is cast down . . . (12:10) .

This ultimate and complete salvation is called glorifica tion. Paul said, "If so be that we suffer with him [in this life], that we may be also glorified together. For I reckon that the sufferings of this present time are not worthy to be compared with the *glory* which shall be revealed in us" (Rom. 8:17–18; author's italics; cf. 8:30) . As children of God we shall be heirs of God and joint-heirs with Christ (Rom. 8:17) .

We shall share in the glory of Christ in heaven (Rev. 4:11; 5:5–14; 20–21). The eloquent Paul, even when writing under inspiration, could not find words to express it: "But we speak the wisdom of God in a mystery . . . which God ordained before the world unto *our glory:* which none of the princes of this world knew. . . . But as it is written, Eye hath not seen, nor ear heard, neither have entered into the heart of man, the things which God hath prepared for them that love him" (1 Cor. 2:7–9; author's italics).

10

Baptism and the Lord's Supper

Then they that gladly received his word were baptized: and the same day there were added unto them about three thousand souls. And they continued stedfastly in the apostles' doctrine and fellowship, and in breaking of bread, and in prayers.
Acts 2:41–42

In this chapter we consider two of the most disputed of all the practical aspects of Christian doctrine. It is indeed strange that they are disputed, since the teaching of the New Testament regarding them is so clear. It is well, therefore, that we examine carefully both the scriptural and historical matters pertaining to baptism and the Lord's Supper. In doing so, it is hoped that more clarity and insight will be gained regarding these two significant observances.

I. The Two Ordinances

While the Roman Catholic Church has what it calls the seven sacraments, the New Testament church had only two ordinances—baptism and the Lord's Supper. They are not sacramental but symbolic in nature.

1. *The meaning of the word "ordinance."*—Strange to say, the word "ordinance" is never used in the New Testament in direct reference either to baptism or to the Lord's Supper. Six words in the Old Testament are translated ordinance (*choq*, statute, decree, Ex. 12:24; 18:20; Mal. 3:7; *chuqqah*, statute, decree, Ex. 12:14, 17; Job 38:33; *yad*, hand, Ezra 3:10; *mitsvah*, command, charge, precept, Neh. 10:32; *mishmereth*, watch, ward, guard, Lev. 18:30; 22:9; Mal. 3:14; *mishpat*, judgment, Ex. 15:25; Josh. 24:25; Psalm 119:91; Ezek. 11:20). In the New Testament there are five words translated ordinance (*diatagē*, thorough arrangement, Rom. 13:2; *dikaiōma*, a judicial appointment, Luke 1:6; Heb. 9:1, 10; *dogma*, dogma, decree, Eph. 2:15; Col. 2:14; *ktisis*, any made thing, 1 Peter 2:13; *paradosis*, a giving over, 1 Cor. 11:2).

2. *The biblical use of the word.*—In the Bible the word "ordinance" is used to refer to either governmental or divine laws. An ordinance is therefore a decree or a command. It is in the latter sense that the word "ordinance" is used with regard to baptism and the Lord's Supper; both are things which Jesus commanded that believers observe (Matt. 28:19; Luke 22:19; 1 Cor. 11:24 ff.). Actually a Christian ordinance is more than a command. It may be defined as a symbolic act commanded by Jesus to signify that which Christ did to effect salvation from sin.

The passage (1 Cor. 11:2) so often quoted in reference to the ordinances of baptism and the Lord's Supper does not refer to them at all. The Greek word used in this verse may be more properly translated traditions, referring to the teachings which Paul declared to the Corinthian Christians.

II. The Ordinance of Baptism

1. The connotation of the word "baptism."—The word "baptism" comes from the Greek word *baptizo,* which means to dip repeatedly, to immerse, or to submerge. It is the intensive form of *bapto,* which means the same thing. In classical Greek *baptizo* is used of dipping animals or of the sinking of a ship. In Josephus *(Antiquities,* IV, iii, 3) is it used to refer to ducking a person until he is drowned. In the Septuagint (2 Kings 5:14) it is used to refer to Naaman, who "dipped himself seven times in Jordan."

In the New Testament *baptizo* is used in several ways: to cleanse by dipping or submerging oneself in water (Mark 7:4); to wash hands by submerging them in water (Luke 11:38); to be overwhelmed or submerged in calamities or cares (Matt. 20:22–23; Mark 10:38–39). But the principal use of the word in the New Testament is in reference to the rite or ceremony called baptism.

Prior to the Christian era the Jews had a rite called ablution, by which they were ceremonially cleansed. The Mosaic law required a person to bathe the body for certain uncleannesses (Lev. 15:16). Tertullian said that the Jew required almost daily washing or baptism (Mark 7:4; cf. Heb. 9:10). Later, in the second century A.D. the Jews employed baptism for proselytes or Gentiles who embraced the Jewish religion. It is not certain that this custom preceded that date. The mystery religions also had a kind of initiatory rite similar to baptism, but while it could have been borrowed from the early Christians, it carried none of the significance of Christian baptism.

2. The ordinance of baptism in the New Testament.—
This ceremony is first introduced in the New Testament in
connection with the ministry of John the Baptist or the Bap-
tizer (*baptistēs*). The baptism of John was a baptism of repentance, an indication that the person submitting to baptism
had repented of his sins and was ready or willing to accept
the coming kingdom of God (Matt. 3:7–8; Luke 3:7–14).

At this point it is well to point out two nouns used in the
New Testament for baptism. *Baptismos* refers to the act of
being baptized or immersed and is used only four times
(Mark 7:4, 8; Heb. 6:2; 9:10) where it refers to the Jewish
ceremonial cleansing. The word *baptisma* denotes the significance or meaning involved in the act of baptism. It appears twenty-two times in the New Testament. Thirteen
times it refers to John's baptism, which had the significance
of repentance (Matt. 3:7; 21:25; Mark 1:4; 11:30; Luke 3:3;
7:29; 20:4; Acts 1:22; 10:37; 13:24; 18:25; 19:3–4). Five
times it refers to Jesus' baptism or immersion into the calam-
ity of the cross (Matt. 20:22–23; Mark 10:38–39; Luke 12:50).
Four times it refers to Christian baptism (Rom. 6:4; Eph.
4:5; Col. 2:12; 1 Peter 3:21). That John's baptism was not
synonymous with Christian baptism is seen in Acts 19:3–5.
The disciples of John the Baptist had received the baptism
with respect to repentance, but they knew nothing of the
significance of Christian baptism.

The question naturally arises as to why Jesus submitted to
baptism (Matt. 3:16), since it certainly was not to signify
repentance in Jesus' case. Three things are signified by Jesus'
baptism: He authenticated the ministry of John; he set an example for his followers; he publicly dedicated himself for his
own ministry which would end in his death, burial, and resurrection. Jesus' baptism thus marked the transition of the
significance of baptism (*baptisma*) from merely repentance

and acceptance of the kingdom of God to that which Christians symbolize in it, the redemptive work of Jesus Christ.

The ceremony of Christian baptism (*baptisma*), then, is a symbol of the death, burial, and resurrection of Jesus, of that which he did for our salvation (Matt. 20:22–23). In submitting to baptism we also testify to death to the old life, burial, and resurrection to walk in newness of life in Christ (Rom. 6:4–6; Col. 2:12). It also implies faith in the coming resurrection from the dead (1 Cor. 15:13 ff.).

3. The significance of baptism in the New Testament.— Keeping in mind that baptism (*baptisma*) refers to the thing implied in the act, we shall deal with the meaning of baptism and the mode of baptism.

First, note the meaning of New Testament baptism. Negatively, it is not necessary for salvation. Late in the second and early in the third centuries the idea of baptismal regeneration began to appear. Even in the first century certain heretical teachers sought to add other things to faith as further requirements for salvation (Acts 15; cf. Gal.). Some sought to impose upon the simple Christian faith the observance of rites connected with Judaism (Col. 2:16–23). But all these the early Christians rejected (Acts 15:23–29). However, error does not die so easily. This error, among many others, finally evolved into what history knows as the Roman Catholic Church. Beginning, therefore, in the second and third centuries, the idea of baptismal regeneration gradually became an accepted teaching of that group. Happily, however, there persisted a minority, somewhat underground, group which continued to practice the New Testament faith. This group later came to be known as Baptist.

However, this error has persisted even to the present time, both in Catholicism and most branches of Protestantism. The greater number of the latter groups hold that there is a grace to be received in baptism that cannot be found elsewhere. To that extent they believe in baptismal regeneration. But some, such as the Church of Christ and the Disciples of Christ (Christian Church), along with Catholics, insist that baptism is necessary for salvation. Such belief is based upon certain proof texts to the neglect of the over-all teaching of the New Testament. One such text is Mark 16:16: "He that believeth and is baptized shall be saved; but he that *believeth* not shall be damned" (author's italics). Suffice it to say that the oldest and most reliable manuscripts of Mark end with 16:8. The remainder is probably a later addition. Note that this addition also includes snake handling and poison drinking as evidences of faith (16:18). Even if this verse is accepted as genuine Scripture, notice that 16:16 says nothing about the individual's being damned if he is not baptized.

Another proof text is Acts 2:38: "Repent, and be baptized . . . *for* the remission of sins" (author's italics). The word "for" translates the Greek preposition *eis,* which may variably be translated for, into, at, because of, or on the basis of, according to its use in the sentence. A. T. Robertson, the leading Greek scholar of the twentieth century, said that this preposition should be translated in Acts 2:38 as at, because of, on the basis of, or as a result of. In Luke 11:32 exactly the same usage of *eis* is translated: "For they [Nineveh] repented *at* the preaching of Jonas" (author's italics). The people of Nineveh repented not for, into, or in order that Jonah might preach but as the result of his preaching. So Peter said, in effect, "Repent and be baptized as the result of or on the basis of the remission of sins." This translation fits exactly the broad teaching of the New Testament!

Note that Jesus did all that was necessary for salvation, yet we are expressly told that he baptized no one (John 4:2). Paul, the apostle to the Gentiles, said that he was sent not to baptize but to preach the gospel (1 Cor. 1:14–17). The New Testament abounds in instances of and statements about salvation with no reference to baptism (Luke 23:42–43; John 3:16; 5:24; Acts 16:31).

Furthermore, baptism is not to be administered to infants. Because men believed in baptismal regeneration, they began to baptize infants. Suffice it to say that there is not one shred of evidence in the New Testament to support infant baptism. Nor is it to be administered to the living for the dead. One verse (1 Cor. 15:29) is cited for this practice: "Else what shall they do which are baptized for the dead?" Some translate this verse "baptized with respect to dead works." Even if "dead" refers to people, the practice is expressly repudiated.

Baptism is to be administered only to those who have experienced an inward change by a conscious acceptance of Jesus as Saviour (Acts 16:31–33). John the Baptist refused baptism to the Sadducees and Pharisees who knew no repentance (Matt. 3:7–9). Peter demanded repentance as the basis for baptism (Acts 2:38). Acts 2:41 says, "They that *gladly received* his word were baptized" (author's italics). Paul baptized the Philippian jailer after he had believed on the Lord Jesus Christ and was saved (Acts 16:30–33). While baptism is not necessary for salvation, it is an act of obedience (Matt. 28:19) by which we show that our faith for salvation is in the death, burial, and resurrection of Jesus Christ and that we have died to sin, the old life has been buried, and we are raised to a new life in Christ. "Know ye not, that so many of us as were baptized into [*eis,* with respect to] Jesus Christ were baptized into [*eis,* with respect to] his death? Therefore we are buried with him by baptism into [*eis*] death [as the result of death]: that like as Christ was raised up from the dead by the glory of the Father, even so we also should walk in [*en*] newness of life" (Rom. 6:3–4).

Now let us consider the mode of New Testament baptism. The meaning of baptism determines the mode. Negatively, again we note that baptism is not pouring water on the body. Because some early Christians believed in baptismal regeneration, the practice of pouring came into vogue for both health and convenience. In cases of sickness it was thought best not to immerse the body but simply to pour water on the candidate. Likewise, it was more convenient since it required less water. Finally this practice was simplified into pouring water on the head only. The first mention of such practice is in the *Teaching of the Twelve Apostles,* which is dated in the second century. It states that proper baptism is in living water; if living water is not available, then in other water; in cold water, but if not, in warm water. "But if thou hast neither, pour water upon the head thrice" in the name of the Trinity. There is a Greek word for pour (*epicheō*) which the New Testament writers could have used had this been the proper method.

Nor is baptism sprinkling water on the head. The transition from pouring to sprinkling was simple. If the amount of water was not important, sprinkling was more convenient and better for infants and sick people. This practice began about the middle of the third century A.D. But again there is a Greek word for sprinkle (*rantizo*) which is never used in connection with baptism. Thus in both pouring and sprinkling the meaning of baptism has been destroyed; or better still, the meaning has been changed from symbol to sacrament and thus the mode has lost its meaning.

Positively, we declare that New Testament baptism is immersion in water and emergence from water. Only thus do we portray the meaning of baptism! This mode is abundantly supported by the Greek language. We have noted the meaning of the Greek verb *baptizo:* dip, plunge, submerge, immerse. In this regard it is interesting to note that when the Catholic Church split into the Roman and Greek Orthodox groups, the Greek Orthodox Church retained immersion as its form of baptism. The English word *baptize* is not a translation but a transliteration of the Greek word, done in the King James Version by scholars in A.D. 1611. These scholars found refuge in transliteration; everyone could read into the word his own meaning.

Furthermore, immersion is supported by Christian history. In the early 1940's, while digging in the marshes outside the city of Rome, workmen unearthed the remains of a Christian church dating back to the second century A.D. In it they found a baptistery with plumbing intact! In Florence, Italy, the oldest building is the Baptistery, dating back to the eleventh century. It was the place of baptism. In it today is a large baptistery in which Dante was baptized. Built into its top is a smaller baptistery where babies were baptized. On the walls of the Baptistery is a large mural painting of John immersing Jesus in the Jordan.

Sprinkling did not become the official mode of Roman Catholic baptism until the thirteenth century A.D. Therefore, in all Catholic churches in Europe built before that time, if there are paintings or mosaics showing Jesus' baptism, they always picture immersion. In fact, Roman Catholics simply admit that they changed the mode.

Again, immersion is supported by Christian scholarship. No Baptist has written a lexicon of the Greek language, yet all standard lexicons give the meaning of *baptizo* as dip, immerse. None gives pour or sprinkle, nor has anyone ever found an instance where the word means pour or sprinkle. John Calvin said, "The very word baptize, however, signifies to immerse." Marcus Dods said, "To use Pauline language, his old man is dead and buried in the water, and he rises from this cleansing grave a new man. The full significance of the rite would have been lost had immersion not been practised . . . a rite wherein by immersion in water the participant symbolizes and signalizes his transition from an impure to a pure life, his death to a past he abandons, and his new birth to a future he desires." Alfred Plummer wrote that the office of John the Baptist was "to bind them to a new life, symbolized by an immersion in water." Lightfoot stated that "Baptism is the grave of the old man, and the birth of the new. As he sinks beneath the baptismal waters, the believer buries there all his corrupt affections and past sins; as he emerges thence, he rises regenerate, quickened to new hopes and new life."

Concerning the recipients of baptism, note the following. Jacobus wrote, "We have no record in the New Testament of the baptism of infants." Scott wrote, "The New Testament contains no explicit reference to the baptism of infants or young children." Plummer said, "The recipients of Christian baptism were required to repent and believe."

In summary we quote Sanday and Headlam in their *Commentary on Romans*. "It [baptism] expresses *symbolically* a series of acts corresponding to the redeeming acts of Christ. Immersion = Death. Submersion = Burial (the ratification of death). Emergence = Resurrection." No Baptist could have stated it better! The meaning of baptism is seen in its symbolism of that which Christ taught by example.

4. The Baptist rejection of the baptism of other denominations.—In the case of those who practice sprinkling the reason for rejection is quite clear: the mode is not New Testament baptism. In the case of those who practice immersion *for salvation* (Church of Christ and Disciples of Christ), the meaning is wrong (cf. Acts 19:3–5). Baptists regard baptism by these groups as a perversion of New Testament baptism.

III. The Ordinance of the Lord's Supper

1. The four historic views.—The Roman Catholic view of the Lord's Supper includes transubstantiation. This word means substance across, or that in the Mass the bread and wine actually become the body and blood of Jesus. The Lutheran view is consubstantiation. This means substance with, or that the actual body and blood of Jesus are present with the bread and wine. This is a modification of the Catholic view. Others believe *grace with it,* that one receives grace through taking the elements which is not available otherwise. Baptists believe that the Lord's Supper is a symbol. This simply means that the elements are merely a symbol of the broken body and spilled blood of Jesus.

2. The question of close communion.—Are Baptists "close communionists"? To begin with, communion is not among men but between God and man. The word "communion" (*koinōnia*) means to have all things in common or in fellowship (2 Cor. 6:14; 13:14). The only time that this word is used in connection with the Christian ordinance is in 1 Corinthians 10:16. The reference here (10:16–33) is in a discussion of whether or not the Christians should eat meat offered to idols; Paul was thinking of the Christian's union with Christ. The communion is with Christ, not with man. The New Testament name for this ordinance is "Lord's Supper."

Most Christian groups agree that baptism should precede the Lord's Supper. So say the Baptists. But what is New Testament baptism? Thus the difference is not over the Lord's Supper but over baptism. If anything, therefore, Baptists are close-baptismists.

3. Observing the Lord's Supper.—The Lord did not state when or how often believers should observe the Lord's Supper. He instituted the Supper on Thursday night, but the early Christians observed it on the Lord's Day. Any New Testament baptized believer is eligible to take the Supper. None is worthy but by the grace of God. The word "unworthily" in 1 Corinthians 11:29 is an adverb of manner, referring not to the condition of the person but to the manner in which the Corinthian Christians were observing the Supper. They were making .of it a bacchanalian banquet (11:20–22; Lord's Supper should read lordly supper, or banquets held in honor of Caesar) . The purpose of the Lord's Supper is to remember Christ and what he did for our salvation (1 Cor. 11:24–26) until he comes again.

Thus both baptism and the Lord's Supper are symbols of what Christ did for our salvation. In the New Testament baptism always preceded the Lord's Supper. Baptism is an initiatory rite and is administered only one time. The Lord's Supper is a repetitive act of remembrance and should be observed often in the Christian's life. Both are given by command of Jesus. To neglect either is to be disobedient to his will.

11

The Church

*Upon this rock I will build my church;
and the gates of hell [Hades] shall not
prevail against it.* MATTHEW 16:18

THE CONCEPT OF THE CHURCH looms large
in the New Testament. While this idea is basic in Christian
history, there is a wide difference in particular beliefs of various Christian bodies with regard to the nature of the teachings of the New Testament and as to the ideas involved in
the word. In this, as in many other matters, Baptists are distinct. It is important, therefore, that we give careful study to
the matter of the New Testament doctrine of the church.

I. The Meaning of the Word "Church"

1. The linguistic meaning.—The English word "church"
is a translation of the Greek word *ekklesia*. The word
ekklesia comes from two other Greek words, the preposition
ek, meaning out or out of, and the verb *kalein*, meaning to
call. Thus the word *ekklesia* means those who are called out.

Its general use in Greek was to express the idea of an assembly.

2. The extra-Christian meaning.—In secular Greek the word referred to the duly constituted gathering of the citizens of a self-governing Greek city. In Acts 19:39 it is used to denote such an assembly of the citizens of Ephesus. In this sense it refers to a purely democratic political body. In the Septuagint *ekklesia* translates the Hebrew word *qahal*, referring to the nation of Israel assembled before God (cf. Deut. 31:30, congregation; Judges 21:8, assembly; 1 Chron. 29:1, congregation). In the New Testament two references to this Old Testament idea are found (Acts 7:38, church; Heb. 2:12, church). The Jewish idea of the synagogue (Greek, *sunagoge,* a leading together or a place where people are led together) contains something of this idea.

3. The Christian meaning.—The idea of the *ekklesia* was one with which Jesus' followers were familiar. But Jesus poured into it a peculiar content when he said, "I will build my church [*ekklesia*]." The disciples were familiar with the word both in its religious and political relationships. In essence, Jesus said, "The Hebrews have their assembly, and the Greeks have theirs. Now I will build my assembly." The Hebrew concept was that of the assembly of all of God's people before him and under his theocratic rule. The Greek concept was that of a local segment of people assembled in democratic deliberation to solve their own problems, but under the guidance of those principles inherent in democratic government. In the New Testament the church is a "theocratic democracy" (Lindsay), a society of those who are free but always conscious that their freedom springs from loyalty to Christ. This is a body of those who are brought together through their love for Christ and whose liberty is in loving obedience to him.

II. The Twofold Nature of the Church

The word *ekklesia* is used 115 times in the New Testament. At least ninety-two times it refers to the local church. While the other uses are not inconsistent with this idea, they more definitely refer to the church in a general sense.

1. The general idea of the church.—In this sense the word "church" includes all believers in Christ in all ages (Matt. 16:18). It is used in the generic sense to refer to the over-all fellowship of the redeemed without respect to locality or time (Acts 8:1, 3; 12:1; 1 Cor. 15:9; Gal. 1:13; Phil. 3:6) Note, however, that these verses could actually refer to Jerusalem, although the specific references are not to a given congregation. The most general reference to the church is in Ephesians (1:22; 3:10,21; 5:23–32; cf. Col. 1:18, 24; 1 Tim. 3:15), a letter written to be read to several local congregations.

In the general sense the church is not to be confused with organized Christianity or with any particular segment thereof. It is correct to use the term in a general sense only with reference to the church as the inclusion of all those who are in Christ, and as such the church will not exist until after the judgment. Strictly speaking, a church is an assembled group. The assembly of all the redeemed in one place will become a reality only after the return of the Lord and the judgment (cf. Heb. 12:23; Rev. 21–22).

The question of distinction between the church general and the kingdom of God is a worthy one. While some make the church synonymous with the kingdom, a caution is in order. The church general, as composed of all the redeemed, is in the kingdom of God. Actually, the kingdom of God refers to the reign of God over all created things—angels, men, devils, and nature. In the final state following our Lord's re-

turn and the judgment, God will reign over a redeemed creation (Rom. 8:19–22; Rev. 21:1) ; over Satan, his angels, and
the unregenerate in hell (1 Cor. 15:24–28; Phil. 2:10–11;
Rev. 20:10–15) ; and in heaven over the holy angels and the
redeemed of all ages (Rev. 21–22) . When Jesus came, he did
so to establish the reign of God, not only in men's hearts, but
over all things in the universe. Each time a soul submits to
God through Christ that soul enters the kingdom. As such
he also becomes a part of the church general. However, we
may distinguish between the church and the kingdom by
saying that the church, general and local, is that phase of
God's kingdom charged with the extension of his reign
among men. To the church is given the keys of the kingdom.

2. *The local idea of the church.*—Remembering that the
church general will not become a tangible reality until that
time when we are gathered in glory after the judgment, it is
not strange that in the New Testament the greater emphasis
is placed upon the idea of the church in a local sense. Nor is
it any wonder that in practically every case the reference to
the church general may also be applied to the local church.
The local church is the visible operation of the church
general in a given time and place. This idea is seen in Jesus'
first reference to the church: "I will build my church. . . .
And I will give unto thee the keys of the kingdom of heaven"
(Matt. 16:18–19) . Here the church carries the concept of the
general sense, but also that of the local church's using the
"keys of the kingdom of heaven." In Matthew 18:17 Jesus
definitely had in mind the local congregation (cf. 18:18–20) .
The references in Matthew 16 and 18 are Jesus' only uses of
the term "church," while the term "kingdom" was often on
his lips.

One exception should be noted as regards the two ideas of
the church. Whereas we are born again into the church gen-

eral, we are baptized into the local church. To the local church Jesus committed the two ordinances of baptism and the Lord's Supper so that in their observance it might witness to his saving work in a given locality. Thus while salvation is synonymous with membership in the church general, it is not so with regard to the local church, nor is membership in the local church synonymous with salvation.

We repeat, then, that the vast majority of references to the church in the New Testament are in the local sense (Matt. 18:17; Acts 2:47; 5:11; 9:31; 11:26; 14:23; 15:3–4; Rom. 16:1, 4–5, 16, 23; 1 Cor. 1:2; 4:17; 7:17; Gal. 1:2; 1 Thess. 1:1). As such the local church was a democratic assembly, acting under the lordship of Christ and directing its own affairs. The local church chose Judas' successor (Acts 1:15 ff.), selected deacons (Acts 6:1 ff.), administered the ordinances (Acts 2:41–42), approved the work of evangelism (Acts 11:1–18), sent out missionaries (Acts 13:1 ff.), and received reports on mission work (Acts 14:27). While independent, however, by common consent the local churches were interdependent. In deciding matters of doctrine the Antioch and Jerusalem churches conferred together under the guidance of the Holy Spirit (Acts 15; Gal. 2). To aid the churches in Palestine, Paul challenged all the churches elsewhere to cooperate in taking an offering for that purpose (1 Cor. 16:1–4; 2 Cor. 8; cf. Acts 20:4; 1 Cor. 16:3–4; 2 Cor. 8:19–21).

III. Specific Matters Regarding the Local Church

1. The officers of the church.—First, there is the office of bishop, elder, or pastor. In the New Testament these titles refer to the same office with emphasis in each case placed upon a particular phase of duty (see Thayer, *in loco*).

The word "bishop" comes from the Greek word *episkopos*, meaning overseer or, in Greek life, one charged with the

duty of seeing that things to be done by others are done cor-
rectly. In the New Testament it is used to refer to the one
charged as the overseer of a local church (Acts 20:28; Phil.
1:1; 1 Tim. 3:2; Titus 1:7). It is also used of Christ as the
"overseer" of souls (1 Peter 2:25).

Elder translates the Greek word *presbuteros*, which con-
notes age (Acts 2:17). It came to refer to the dignity associated with age and hence to the dignity of an office. Among
the Jews it referred to members of the Sanhedrin (Matt.
16:21; 26:47, 57, 59), who were usually older men. Among
Christians it denoted those who presided over assemblies of
the church (Acts 11:30; 14:23; 15:2, 4, 6, 22 ff.; 1 Tim. 5:17,
19; Titus 1:5; 2 John 1). Thayer's Greek *Lexicon* has this
to say:

That they [elders] did not differ at all from the (*episkopoi*)
bishops or overseers (as is acknowledged also by Jerome on Tit.
1:5. . . .) is evident from the fact that the two words are used
indiscriminately, Acts 20:17, 28; Tit. 1:5, 7, and that the duty of
presbyters [elders] is described by the terms *episkopein*, 1 Pet.
5:1 sg., and *episkopē*, Clem. Rom. 1, Cor. 44:1; accordingly only
two ecclesiastical officers, *hoi episkopoi* and *hoi diakonoi*, are distinguished in Phil. 1:1; 1 Tim. 3:1, 8. The title *episkopos* denotes
the function, *presbuteros* the dignity; the former was borrowed
from Greek institutions, the latter from the Jewish. . . ."

(THAYER, p. 536).

"Pastor" is translated from the Greek word *poimēn*, a shepherd. The Greek verb means to feed or tend a flock, as sheep
(Luke 17:7; 1 Cor. 9:7), and applied to men it meant to rule
or govern (Matt. 2:6; Rev. 2:27). It is used to refer to the
overseer or pastor (John 21:16; Acts 20:28; 1 Peter 5:2).

The three words—overseer, elder, and pastor—therefore
refer to the same office. There is no single instance in the
New Testament where "bishop" refers to one over a group

of churches or where "elders," in the Christian sense, refers to an office apart from that of pastor.

The second office is that of deacon. While the title is not given, the office is doubtless described in Acts 6. The word *diakonos* is of questioned origin. One suggested source is a word meaning to execute the commands of another. Probably the word comes from the verb *diakoneō,* meaning to be servant or attendant, to serve or wait upon. Its Latin equivalent, *ministrare,* means to wait at table and offer food and drink to guests. In either event, the word "deacon" means a servant.

The above fits the original service of the deacon (Acts 6). Jesus called himself a deacon (Matt. 20:28) who gave his life as a ransom for lost men. Paul called himself a deacon (Col. 1:25) charged to teach God's Word. In 2 Corinthians 11:15 Paul spoke of Satan's deacons (the reference is to "false apostles"). But the point is clear—the office is that of one who serves. That it came to include more than simply serving tables is most certain. It included service for Christ through the church pertaining to the material as well as the spiritual welfare of the church (Acts 6:8 ff.; 8:5 ff.). In that light we can best understand the qualifications of the deacon (Acts 6:3; 1 Tim. 3:8–13; note the qualifications for a bishop, 1 Tim. 3:1–7, and the similarity of the two). At any rate, the bishops and deacons were closely allied in their work as noted by the twin salutations (Phil. 1:1) and the relationship between their service (Acts 6). When both function properly, the work of the church prospers (Acts 6:7).

In addition, in the New Testament there seem to have been men who were not connected with any local church who functioned in a given capacity according to the gift bestowed upon them by the Holy Spirit (1 Cor. 12:28). There is no instance where these were ordained persons in the sense that the bishops and deacons were. In Ephesians 4:11–12 Paul lists these as apostles, prophets, and evangelists, in addition to pastors and teachers. The apostles were pioneers in inaugurating new work in the broadest sense. This duty fell not only to the twelve but to Paul (Rom. 1:1), Silas and Timothy (1 Thess. 1:1; 2:6), and Barnabas (Acts 14:14). The prophets furnished divine guidance in the new fellowship in its organization, discipline, and function (Acts 13:1–2; 15:32–33). Evangelists seem to have been local or district missionaries whose duty it was to develop the work around the centers established by the apostles (Acts 21:8; 2 Tim. 4:5; see Carver, pp. 149–50).

2. *The democratic nature of each church.*—Already we have noted how each church functioned as an independent body in the furtherance of the gospel. Let us note now the church's function in local affairs. In giving, Paul could exhort the churches, but each church must decide for itself its response (1 Cor. 16:1–4; 2 Cor. 8:1–8, note especially vv. 7–8). In receiving and excluding members each church exercised this local authority. To be sure, the Lord added to the church (Acts 2:47), but the Lord's will was made known through his churches (Acts 13:1–2). It is inherent in the very nature of democratic bodies to determine those who are qualified for membership in them.

We definitely know that the local church had authority to exclude from membership those who proved to be unworthy (Matt. 18:17 ff.). Jesus said that the church gathered together has his presence and acts for him (Note Matt. 18:18; cf. Matt. 16:19). In 2 Thessalonians 3:6 Paul directed the church, "in the name of our Lord Jesus Christ, that ye withdraw [in the name of our Lord Jesus Christ] yourselves from every brother [Christian] that walketh disorderly." In 1 Corinthians 5:4–5 he said, "In the name of our Lord Jesus

Christ, when ye are gathered together . . . with the power of our Lord Jesus Christ, to deliver such an one [immoral person] unto Satan for the destruction of the flesh, that the spirit may be saved." In 2 Corinthians 2:4–11 Paul exhorted this same church to forgive someone who had grieved the church. This is probably the same one mentioned in 1 Corinthians 5:4–5. The right to exclude implies the right to receive.

At this point we shall do well to note the impossibility of an ecumenical church. The New Testament knows no such. Southern Baptists are criticized for not joining in such a movement. The very nature of the Southern Baptist Convention forbids its joining. The National Council of Churches and the World Council of Churches accept only the membership of denominations. The New Testament pattern allows no authoritative organization above the local church. Other Baptist organizations—district associations, state conventions, national conventions, and the world alliance—are composed of messengers from the local church. Such messengers have no delegated authority, and it is the local church which chooses either to co-operate or not to co-operate with the decisions and programs of the other bodies. No central body can commit the local Baptist church; ecumenical movements accept only composite bodies. Hence the local church cannot join; neither can the Southern Baptist Convention commit the local churches to join.

3. The commission of the church.—Keeping in mind the Great Commission (Matt. 28:19–20), let us note once more the first mention of the church by Jesus (Matt. 16:18–19). Following Peter's confession of the messiahship of Jesus, our Lord blessed him, saying that such a revelation came from heaven. Then Jesus said these words: "Thou art Peter [*petros*], and upon this rock [*petra*] I will build my church. . . . And I will give unto thee the keys of the kingdom of heaven: and whatsoever thou shalt bind on earth shall be bound [future perfect passive verb, shall have been bound] in heaven: and whatsoever thou shalt loose on earth shall be loosed [future perfect passive verb, shall have been loosed] in heaven." Note the different words *petros* and *petra*. *Petros* means a stone or fragment of the large rock; *petra* means a ledge rock or foundation stone (Matt. 27:51). The church was not founded upon the *petros* but upon the *petra*. Peter was simply a fragment or stone confessing faith in the ledge rock, or Jesus himself. In this instance Peter, then, is not to be regarded as a person so much as a symbol of all who profess such a faith. The church is built out of "living stones" (*lithos*, small stones, 1 Pet. 2:5), made alive by their confession of faith in Christ, the *petra* or ledge rock.

Note also in Matthew 16:19 that the church is made the steward of the keys of the kingdom. Heaven has already decreed that by its binding or loosing—using or refusing to use the keys—men will be lost or saved. Thus the "eternal purpose" of God in redemption shall be realized "by [through] the church" (Eph. 3:10–11). To no other institution did he give such a responsibility!

Thus the church is called the "body of Christ" (Eph. 1:22–23), with Christ as its Head (1 Cor. 11:3; Eph. 4:15; Col. 1:18; 2:19). In 1 Corinthians 12 Paul developed this idea completely, showing that all Christians are particular members of the body with diversified gifts with which to serve Christ. The church is also the "bride of Christ" (John 3:29). This figure is often mentioned in the New Testament (Matt. 9:15; 25:1 ff.; Luke 5:34; Rev. 21:2); it suggests love and fruitfulness. The bride joins with the Holy Spirit in calling men to come to Jesus (Rev. 22:17). Again the church is called the "pillar and ground," or "stay," of the truth (1 Tim. 3:15). Here again we see the church as the custodian of the gospel. Thus the church is the body of Christ to carry out his orders under the direction of the Head; it is the bride of Christ to be loved by him and to love him as in travail it brings forth spiritual children; it is the pillar and ground of the truth to declare the whole counsel of God.

The church, then, is both universal and local. Since the church universal will not be a reality until all the redeemed assemble in glory, the local church is a little "colony of heaven" (Phil. 3:20), a "sounding board" of the gospel (1 Thess. 1:8), and a fellowship (Acts 2:42) through which we are to carry out our stewardship of the gospel to all men. Since the church is local, it is the only institution through which we can serve. The person who despises the church despises Christ, for it is his body and bride.

12

Death, Resurrection, Heaven, and Hell

It is appointed unto men once to die, but after this the judgment: so Christ was once offered to bear the sins of many; and unto them that look for him shall he appear the second time without sin unto salvation. HEBREWS 9:27–28

IN ONE SENSE, in this discussion we are dealing with the doctrine of last things, which will be considered at length in the next chapter. However, before passing to that subject in its broader aspects we shall do well to limit this treatment to some specific matters.

I. The Reality of Death

1. The general teachings of the Bible.—The idea of death is first presented in Genesis 2:17 when Adam was warned against disobeying God in eating the forbidden fruit. "For in the day that thou eatest thereof thou shalt surely die." Reflection on this warning reveals death in two aspects—physical and spiritual. That Adam and Eve did not die physically on the day of disobedience is evident, for Adam was 930 years old when he died. The immediate death was spiritual; the further consequence of sin was physical death. It is important to note this sequence. The fact is that when God made man in his own image (Gen. 1:27; 2:7) he made him to live forever, spiritually and physically. The Scriptures and man's experience tell a sordid story of death in both realms.

The word translated "death" (Hebrew, *maweth;* Greek, *thanatos*) means a separation and is so used to indicate spiritual or physical death. When the spirit dwells in the physical body, there is physical life. When the spirit is separated from the body, the body is dead. But in no sense does the Bible speak of this separation as the end of man (Gen. 25:11; cf. Matt. 22:32; Matt. 17:3; Luke 16:22). Spiritual death is the separation of the soul from God (Eph. 2:1).

In the New Testament the Greek word for death (*thanatos,* Thayer) is used in three ways: the death of the body or the separation of the soul from the body by which earthly life is ended (John 11:4; Acts 2:24; Phil. 2:27, 30); the loss of that life which alone is worthy of the name, the misery of soul which results from the separation of the soul from God by sin, beginning on earth but continuing and increasing after the death of the body (Rom. 7:13; 2 Cor. 3:7; 7:10; cf. Luke 16:19 ff.); the miserable state of the wicked dead in hell (Rom. 1:32; Rev. 20:14; 21:8). All are the fruit of sin (Gen. 2:17; 1 Cor. 15:21–22, 56).

2. Specific matters concerning physical and spiritual death. —While the major emphasis of the Bible is on spiritual death, it does take cognizance of physical death (Gen. 21:16; 25:11; 27:2; 2 Sam. 1:1; Psalms 13:3; 23:4; Matt. 10:21; 16:28; 26:66;

1 Cor. 3:22). Death is the common experience of all men except Enoch (Gen. 5:24) and Elijah (2 Kings 2:11). In the Old Testament death was looked upon with more dread than in the New Testament (Job 10:21; 26:6; 28:13; Psalm 88:10–13; Isa. 38:11, 18–19). However, even in the Old Testament some light appears (Deut. 5:26; 32:39; Josh. 3:10; 1 Sam. 2:6; Job 14:13 ff.; Psalm 139:7–8; Isa. 38:5; Ezek. 37:11–12; Dan. 12:2; Hos. 6:2).

It is of interest to note that the New Testament does not regard physical death as necessarily an evil within itself. Though the death of Christ is presented as his saving work, even he did not draw back from death. His prayer in Gethsemane was not regarding the act of dying but what it contained—his becoming sin (Matt. 26:39). Jesus called the physical death of Lazarus "sleep" (John 11:11–14; cf. Mark 5:39; Acts 7:60; 1 Thess. 4:13). In his raising Lazarus from the dead the prime motive was not positive good for the deceased but the grief of the bereaved (Mark 5:22–23, 38; Luke 7:11 ff.; John 11:33 ff.). Paul caught something of Jesus' attitude when he said, "For to me to live is Christ, and to die is gain" (Phil. 1:21 ff.; cf. Rom. 8:35 ff.). The early Christians did not fear death (Acts 4:29; 7:55–60; 2 Tim. 4:6 ff.).

But even so, since death is the fruit of sin, it is regarded as an enemy (1 Cor. 15:26). However, God causes his enemies to serve him as he works in all things, even death, for good to those who love him (Rom. 8:28). Suppose that man, subject to the frailties entailed by sin, could not die! God even makes this enemy to serve him and us that we might be delivered from this corruptible body to inherit an incorruptible one (Rom. 7:24–25; 1 Cor. 15:50 ff.).

The greater emphasis in the New Testament is placed upon spiritual death. Of interest is the contrast between the human and the biblical concept of death. While the Bible regards physical death less seriously than spiritual death, man does just the opposite. If a child is lost from his parents, we show great concern, but we are too often indifferent to the plight of the child lost from God. We would be wise to gauge our concern by the Bible's concern.

Earlier we noted that Adam died spiritually before he died physically. This is ever true. Even while men are alive in the flesh they are often dead in sin (Eph. 2:1 ff.; cf. Luke 15:24). The soul that is separated from God by sin is dead, though actually the soul is immortal (John 5:24; 6:50; 8:21, 24). In this light we also understand Jesus' words in John 11. Lazarus was dead physically, a state which awaits all men except those who are alive at the second coming of Christ (1 Thess. 4:17). Jesus' promise is that those who are alive spiritually shall never die spiritually (John 11:25–26). Thus physical death is shorn of its terror (1 Cor. 15:55–57).

3. The intermediate state.—The intermediate state is the period between physical death and the resurrection. At death the physical body returns to the earth (1 Cor. 15:47; cf. Gen. 3:19; Job 7:21; Psalms 22:15, 29; 104:29) and the soul goes into Hades. The word "Hades" in the New Testament is practically equivalent to "Sheol" in the Old Testament. It means simply the abode or realm of the dead and has no reference to their moral state. Good and evil alike enter into Hades. It is neither Paradise nor Gehenna, but it may be either. Jesus entered Hades (Acts 2:31), as did the rich man in the parable (Luke 16:23). Note that in this parable both Lazarus and the rich man were in Hades, but separated (Luke 16:26). One enjoyed bliss; the other endured suffering (Luke 16:25). Unfortunately, both the words "Hades" and "Sheol" are translated in the King James Version as hell (Psalm 16:10). Most uses of "Sheol" refer to punishment or to the dread of death; but "Hades" always refers to the realm of the dead (cf. Matt. 11:23; 16:18; Luke 10:15; 16:23; Acts 2:27, 31; Rev. 1:18; 6:8; 20:13–14). The New Testament uses another word for hell.

But the New Testament is quite clear as to the distinction between the righteous and the wicked dead in Hades. Jesus referred to the righteous dead such as Abraham, Isaac, and Jacob as "living" (Matt. 22:32). He pictured Lazarus in Hades as being "comforted" in Abraham's bosom (Luke 16:22, 25). To the dying thief Jesus promised, "Today shalt thou be with me in Paradise" (Luke 23:43). To Martha he said that those who lived and believed in him should never die (John 11:26; cf. 2 Cor. 5:1; Phil. 1:23). According to Revelation 6:9–11, the spirits of the departed dead are conscious as they call on God. Peter spoke of the wicked dead as being "in prison" (1 Peter 3:19). In the parable of the rich man and Lazarus (Luke 16:19 ff.) Jesus said of the rich man, "and in hell [Hades] he lift up his eyes, *being in torments,* and seeth Abraham *afar off,* and Lazarus in his bosom. And he cried and said, Father Abraham, have mercy on me . . . for *I am tormented* in this flame" (author's italics). In 2 Peter 2:9 we read that God keeps the unrighteous under punishment "unto the day of judgment."

From these brief references, therefore, we conclude that all the dead go immediately into Hades, the realm of the dead, where they remain in a conscious state. "There is a great gulf fixed: so that they which would pass from hence to you cannot; neither can they pass to us, that would come from thence" (Luke 16:26). At death the Christian goes into Hades but also immediately into the presence of Christ and of God (Luke 16:22; 23:43; Phil. 1:23). They remain in a conscious state of uninterrupted fellowship with Christ (Rom. 8:38–39). They are in a state of happiness and rest (Phil. 1:23; Rev. 14:13). There is no scriptural basis for "soul sleeping," souls of the dead remaining in a state of un-consciousness until the resurrection; or for purgatory, wherein the souls of Christians are purged of sin before entering heaven (cf. Luke 16:26).

The intermediate state is not the final one for believers. The New Testament does not regard this as the final or per-fect state (2 Cor. 5:2–4). Since man is body as well as spirit, Paul longed for the resurrection from the dead (Phil. 3:11). But the immediate state is more blessed in fellowship with Christ than this earthly life (Phil. 1:23). Even so, it is but a foretaste of the final glory of the redeemed (Isa. 64:4; 1 Cor. 2:9).

At death the unrighteous go immediately into Hades, where they remain conscious and begin to endure the penalty for their sins (Luke 16:23 ff.). While the rich man was con-scious of the difference between his state and that of Lazarus, Lazarus did not seem to be aware of the rich man's suffering. Also, the rich man remembered the joys of earth in contrast to his present state and that he had unsaved brothers back on earth, while Lazarus seemed to have no memory of his earthly trials, which were lost in his present bliss. It would appear, therefore, that the saved have no awareness of the lost and doomed state of their acquaintances. This is the answer to the question often asked: "How can I be perfectly happy in heaven if I know of loved ones in hell?" Even if we are aware of those in hell, we shall be so engulfed in the will of God that we shall recognize the rightness of all his judgment. A merci-ful God takes care of the problem.

II. The Fact of the Resurrection

The desire for immortality is inherent in the human heart. The book of Job is probably the oldest book in the Old Testa-ment. In it we hear man's cry, "If a man die, shall he live again?" (14:14). The prophets answered this question in part (Isa. 26:19; Ezek. 37:1–14; Dan. 12:2). It is in the New Testament, however, that the clearest answer is given. To the Sadducees, who denied the resurrection of the body, Jesus declared the fact of the resurrection (Matt. 22:23–33; Mark 12:18–27; Luke 20:27–40; cf. Matt. 8:11; Luke 13:28–29). The Gospel of John clearly teaches it (5:25–29; 11:23 ff.). Acts (1:3; 2:30 ff.; 17:18; 22:7 ff.; 24:15) and the Epistles (Rom. 1:4; 8:11; 1 Cor. 15; Eph. 2:5–6; Col. 2:20; 3:4) abundantly declare it. All New Testament teachings of the resurrection are based on Jesus' resurrection (1 Cor. 15:12 ff.). The word translated resurrection (*anastasis*), meaning a raising up or rising as from the dead, comes from the verb *anistēmi,* which means to stand again or a second time. In this sense it refers to something dead which is made to live again.

1. *The spiritual and physical aspects of the resurrection.*— Some declare that the resurrection refers to the soul but not to the body. While there are references which refer to the immortality of the spirit (John 11:23–26; Eph. 2:1, 5–6; Col. 2:13; Rev. 20:4), in the strictest sense resurrection can refer only to the body. For something to be resurrected it must first be dead. In a bodily resurrection the immortal soul is again clothed in a resurrected body (2 Cor. 5:3–4).

2. *The nature of the resurrected body.*—Paul was curious about the nature of the resurrected body. He asked, "How are the dead raised up? and with what body do they come?" (1 Cor. 15:35). He then proceeded to point out that the resurrected body will be as different from the natural body as the harvest from the seed (vv. 36–38). It will exceed the natural body in glory as celestial bodies exceed terrestrial (vv. 40–42). It will be a body perfectly adapted to the sphere of spiritual living as the bodies of men, beasts, fishes, and birds are adapted to theirs (v. 39). It will be an incorruptible body

(vv. 42 ff.) , not subject to pain or death (Rev. 21:4) . We can best understand this problem as we see the resurrected body of Jesus. His was a bodily resurrection (Luke 24:41 ff.; John 20:20, 27; Acts 10:41) with a body similar to the one he had before his death. Yet it was different, since it was no longer subject to the natural laws of time and space (Matt. 28:2 ff.; Luke 24:15–31, 34; John 20:19) . The best that John could do in describing the resurrection body was to say that "we know that, when he shall appear, we shall be like him" (1 John 3:2) .

III. Heaven and Hell

1. The Bible's teaching concerning heaven.—The Hebrew word for heaven (*shamayim*) means heaved up things (Gen. 1:1; cf. 1:6–8) . The Hebrews thought of a plurality of heavens. Later Jewish literature spoke of seven, with the highest (*aravoth*) being the location of the throne of God. In the other heavens dwelt various superhuman beings, with the second heaven as the abode of evil spirits and angels awaiting punishment (cf. Eph. 6:12) . It is probable that the third heaven was Paradise (2 Cor. 12:2) . The Greek word for heaven (*ouranos*) carried three meanings: the aerial heavens where clouds and birds are (Luke 4:25; 9:54) ; the starry heavens (Mark 13:25; Heb. 11:12) ; and the highest heaven, out of sight, where God dwells (Matt. 5:34; 23:22; Rev. 4:1) . Bible teachings about heaven are restrained. The Bible does not tell us all that we wish to know, but it does tell us all that we need to know. It exhausts language in describing heaven's glory (1 Cor. 2:9) . The language is largely symbolic so that we know that the reality is greater than the symbol.

Outwardly, heaven is a place and not merely a state of being. Jesus said, "I go to prepare a place for you" (John 14:2) .

This place cannot be located. Some believe that the whole universe, redeemed and recreated, will be necessary for our heritage. But it will be where God, who is omnipresent, and Christ are and that will be enough! It will be a glorious place. Gold and precious stones (Rev. 21:18 ff.) suggest moral values; white robes (Rev. 6:11) suggest purity; there will be leaves for healing (Rev. 22:2) and crowns for victory (Rev. 4:10; 19:12). The "unclean" will not be there (Rev. 21:27; Mullins, p. 484).

Inwardly, heaven means (according to Mullins, pp. 485 ff.) relief. In God's presence (Rev. 21:13) we shall be free from those things which make life hard: sorrow, tears, pain, and death (Rev. 21:4). It means reward. Reward is prominent in the picture of heaven. Rewards will be by degrees in keeping with service (Matt. 25:14–30; Luke 19:12–27). Some will be saved "as by fire" (1 Cor. 3:14–15); their works will be burned. To all is promised victory over sin and Satan. In Revelation 2 and 3 rewards for all are set forth.

Heaven will also mean realization. The frustrations and limitations of this life imply a great realization of all our aspirations and desires in heaven. The "white stone" (Rev. 2:17) probably means fulness of personality. Furthermore, there will be fulness of knowledge (1 Cor. 13:8–10); ideal service (Rev. 22:3–4) and worship (Rev. 21:22); perfect fellowship with God in an ideal society (Heb. 12:22–23; Rev. 7:4–11); holiness of character (Rev. 3:5; 21:27); fulness of life (Matt. 25:46); and fellowship with Christ (John 14:3; Rev. 3:21; 5:12–13; 7:17).

Heaven will mean appreciation. In heaven we shall sing the song of Moses and the Lamb (Rev. 15:3). Christ is worthy of praise and honor (Rev. 5:9–12). Christ will give crowns to the victors who, in turn, will cast them at his feet (Rev. 4:10–11).

Heaven will mean endless growth. The standard of greatness which we shall achieve in heaven calls for endless growth (1 Cor. 13:12; Eph. 3:18–19). With the hindrances of the flesh removed, we shall go on growing in grace and in the knowledge of Christ in an endless eternity.

It is well at this point to note in passing the similarity between Genesis 2:8–25 (cf. Gen. 3:17 ff.) and Revelation 22:1–5. It would appear that God closed his Book by describing heaven as a restoration of the conditions of Eden.

2. *The Bible's teaching concerning hell.*—While most people, except the extreme materialists, admit to some idea of heaven, many deny the reality of hell. Yet Jesus said more about hell than he did about heaven. The denial of the existence of hell is due more to wishful thinking and sentimental reasoning than to an interpretation of the factual teaching of the Scripture. To wish there were no hell does not make it so. To say that a merciful God would not make a hell is to examine only one facet of God's nature. Actually God sends no man to hell; he goes there in spite of all God has done to prevent it.

But what are the facts? We have noted that the word "Hades" is translated hell but refers to the grave or realm of the dead without respect to moral condition (Matt. 11:23; 16:18; Luke 16:23; Rev. 1:18). The word translated "hell" that denotes a place of punishment is *gehenna,* the Greek name for the Vale of Hinnom, a valley located south and east of Jerusalem (Josh. 15:8; Matt. 5:22, 29–30; 10:28; 18:9; 23:15, 33; Mark 9:43, 45, 47; Luke 12:5; James 3:6). The Jews so abhorred this place after human sacrifices were abolished by Josiah (2 Kings 23:10) that they used it as a garbage dump into which was cast all the refuse of Jerusalem, including dead animals and the unburied bodies of executed criminals. To consume the garbage, fires burned there day and night without ceasing, maggots worked constantly, and wild dogs howled and fought over the bodies.

To present a picture of hell Jesus adopted this familiar and despised scene. One cannot mistake the imagery of Jesus' warning as he warned men against hell: "the fire that never shall be quenched: where their worm dieth not, and the fire is not quenched" (Mark 9:43–44). "And shall cast them into a furnace of fire: there shall be wailing and gnashing of teeth" (Matt. 13:42). "Outer darkness" and "weeping and gnashing of teeth" could scarcely be misunderstood by a Jew in Jerusalem (Matt. 8:12; 22:13; 25:30).

Thus we have the gruesome picture of hell. Revelation 20:10,14–15 pictures it as a lake of fire. Into it will be cast the devil and his angels (Matt. 25:41) and all whose names are not written in the Book of Life. This is called the second death, or eternal separation of lost souls from God. While it is not located by the Bible, we may be sure that hell is a place as heaven is a place. However, these are only symbols. This is not to deny that hell is a literal fire. The thought to note is that as heaven is more wonderful than symbols can picture it, so hell is more terrible than its symbols describe it. If hell is not fire, it is something infinitely worse. No wonder Jesus warned against it so often and so emphatically! No wonder that God paid such a price to save men from it!

We should remember that as there will be degrees of reward in heaven, so there will be degrees of punishment in hell (Luke 12:47–48). There will be greater punishment for the person who sins against a knowledge of Christ (Matt. 11:21–24) than for the ignorant savage who never heard of him. But both will be there (Rom. 2:6, 12, 15; 4:15). As there will be eternal life in heaven, so there will be eternal punishment in hell (Matt. 25:46).

In summary, all men are appointed to die physically. Outside of Christ all men are dead spiritually even while they are alive physically. For the Christian, physical death is but a passage from time into eternity without a cessation of eternal life or of fellowship with Christ. At the second coming of Christ there will be a resurrection followed by the judgment. Here the saved will be glorified because of their faith and rewarded according to their works; the unsaved will be condemned because of their unbelief and sentenced according to their works. Heaven is the eternal home of the saved; hell is the eternal abode of the lost. Such knowledge should make of each of us a flaming evangel for Christ!

13

Eschatology or Last Things

And this gospel of the kingdom shall be preached in all the world for a witness unto all nations; and then shall the end come. MATTHEW 24:14

THIS SEEMINGLY CLEAR and innocent verse is the center about which swirls a storm of controversy in theological thought, for it points to the end of the world. Volumes almost without number have been written dealing with details of the end of time. About this idea has grown up a system of thought known as eschatology, or the doctrine of last things. We shall discover that from this prism are refracted many shades of thought. No one treatment could be said to represent what any particular group believes about this matter. Actually there are almost as many beliefs about eschatology as there are students of the subject. However, these ideas may be gathered about certain systems of interpretation. To give them in detail would be impossible in so short a space as that allotted to this study. Within the framework of the many shades of thought, however, the basic elements are to be found. It would be impossible to give a treatment of eschatology which would find a general acceptance.

The word "eschatology" comes from the two Greek words *eschatos,* meaning last, and *logos,* meaning reason or science. Thus eschatology is the science of last things. In many uses of the word *eschatos* the reference is simply to last as opposed to first or former things (Matt. 19:30; 20:8, 12, 14, 16). Again it is used to express the idea of finality (Luke 12:59; John 7:37; 1 Cor. 4:9; 15:8, 26, 52). Its most common use has to do with the end of the age (John 6:39–40; 11:24; 12:48; 2 Tim. 3:1; James 5:3; 1 Peter 1:5; 2 Peter 3:3; 1 John 2:18, Jude 18). The science of last things, however, is not confined to those passages in which the word itself appears. In fact, the word "eschatology" does not appear in the New Testament, but it can be noted that the idea is very prevalent in its teachings.

I. The Second Coming of Christ

1. The meaning of the coming of Christ.—We know, of course, that Christ came the first time in his incarnation (John 1:14). During his ministry he spoke of other comings apart from his final appearance. Actually any great intervention of God in Christ in history may be interpreted as a coming of Christ. In this manner Christ referred to his resurrection and that which should follow (Matt. 16:28; 26:64; note that in the latter verse "hereafter" does not mean some future time but "from now on," cf. Broadus); the coming of the Holy Spirit (John 14:18); his coming for the Christian at death (John 14:3); and perhaps the destruction of Jerusalem (Matt. 24:34). The event commonly referred to in Christian thought as the second coming of Christ (Matt. 25:31; Titus 2:13) is the final appearance of Christ at the end of the world. It is to this that we shall confine our examination.

2. *The second coming of Christ.*—Negatively, let us consider false signs of his coming. In his Olivet discourse (Matt. 24–25) Jesus warned against false signs of his return. To the disciples' threefold question (24:3) Jesus replied, "Take heed that no man deceive you" (v. 4). He then listed several false signs that men will use in such deception: false messiahs (vv. 5, 24); wars and rumors of wars (v. 6); and famines, earthquakes, and pestilences (v. 7). The import of this warning is that men shall point to the normal happenings of history as signs of his coming. But we are not to be deceived thereby. Life will go its normal way, of which these things are a part, until without warning Christ will appear (24:37–39). That this caution is needed may be seen by the resurgence of interest in the second coming attendant upon every disturbance in nature or history.

Positively, we may declare that the second coming of Christ is an assured fact. As the Old Testament abounds in prophecies of his first coming, so does the New Testament abound in promises of our Lord's return (Matt. 13:24–30, 36–43, 47–50; 16:27; 24:3–51; 1 Cor. 1:7–8; 15:23–24; 1 Thess. 4:13–18; Heb. 9:28; for a more complete list see Hodges, p. 194) In the first century, as today, many doubted his return (2 Peter 3:1–13), but "the Lord is not slack concerning his promise" (v. 9).

The time of Christ's coming is unrevealed. As he came the first time in the "fulness of time" (Gal. 4:4), so will be the second coming (Matt. 24:28). When conditions are right, he will come. That time Jesus himself did not know (Matt. 24:36; Mark 13:32). He cautioned his disciples against efforts to determine it (Acts 1:7). From Acts 1:8, 11 we judge that our duty is to preach the gospel throughout the earth. In that connection alone do we have any certain word of Jesus as to the time of his coming (Matt. 24:14).

The second coming of Christ will be outward, visible, and personal. This the angels promised: "This same Jesus, which is taken up from you into heaven, shall so come in like manner as ye have seen him go into heaven" (Acts 1:11). Some insist that it will be merely a spiritual coming, but the Scriptures would seem to teach otherwise. The emphasis there is on a personal, bodily return (Matt. 24:29–31; 1 Thess. 4:16). Therefore, the return of the Lord should be the object of constant expectancy. "Therefore be ye also ready: for in such an hour as ye think not the Son of man cometh" (Matt. 24:44). Such expectancy is repeatedly taught by precept and parable (Matt. 24:45–51; 25).

Jesus' coming is described as like that of a thief (Matt. 24:43; 1 Thess. 5:2, 4; 2 Peter 3:10; Rev. 3:3; 16:15). The early Christians lived in daily expectancy of the Lord's return (1 Thess. 4:17; note, "we which are alive"). Some interpret this to mean that Paul was mistaken, thinking that Christ would return during his lifetime. Not so (2 Thess. 2:1–12; cf. 2 Peter 3:3–12)! Paul and others simply lived in daily expectancy. So should we!

3. Problems with respect to the second coming.—These problems hinge largely about a misunderstanding of Jesus' Olivet discourse. Many interpreters take all of Matthew 24–25 (and parallel passages in Mark 13 and Luke 21:5–36) to refer to the second coming. This leads to strained interpretations in many elements of this subject. However, Jesus was here answering three distinct questions: "Tell us, when shall these things be [destruction of Jerusalem, Matt. 24:1–2]? and what shall be the sign of thy coming, and of the end of the world?" (Matt. 24:3). (For a fuller treatment see Hobbs, *Who Is This?*, chapter 10.)

An analysis of this discourse will reveal Jesus' distinct answers to these questions. After warning against false signs (24:4–7; cf. vv. 23–28) and of coming trouble for his followers, Jesus spoke of the destruction of Jerusalem which came in A.D. 70 (24:15–22). After repeating warnings as to false messiahs and signs (24:23–28), he answered the second and third questions (24:29–36). As in verse 28, so in verses 32–33, he pointed out that when conditions are right, he will come. Verse 34 probably refers back to the destruction of Jerusalem. In 24:37–41 Jesus said that life will continue normally until the end. The point here is the surprise element in the second coming, especially on the part of unbelievers, as in the days of Noah. The remainder of the discourse (24:42; 25) deals with exhortations and warnings respecting the second coming.

It is well that we examine the idea of a division of the second coming into two parts. One school of thought teaches two second comings: the first is to be secret or partial, at which time the Lord will take the church to heaven. It will be called the *"rapture."* Those taken at this time will be judged and rewarded, after which they will enjoy a seven-year feast while the Jews endure a period of tribulation. The second part of the second coming will be open and dramatic. The wicked dead shall be raised for the final judgment. The secret coming is based upon such passages as Matthew 24:14–15; Luke 12:39–40; John 14:1–3; 1 Cor. 15:51–52; 1 Thess. 4:13–18; 5:1–4; 2 Thess. 1:6–10; 2 Peter 3:10–12; and Rev. 3:3; 16:15. In all these, however, the import more probably is that of surprise and possibly, in some instances, of separation between the saved and lost.

Of interest is Jesus' warning against belief in a secret coming (Matt. 24:23). "Wherefore if they shall say unto you, Behold, he is in the desert; go not forth: behold, he is in the secret chambers; believe it not. For as the lightning cometh out of the east, and shineth even unto the west; so shall also the coming of the Son of man be" (Matt. 24:26–27). "Behold, he cometh with clouds; and every eye shall see him" (Rev. 1:7). In all probability the Scriptures speak of only one coming, open, dramatic, and with great noise (1 Cor. 15:51–52; 1 Thess. 4:16; 2 Thess. 1:6–10; 2:1–8).

At this juncture we shall do well to look briefly at two words—"rapture" and "tribulation." The term "rapture" refers to the taking up of the resurrected and translated saints to meet the Lord in the air at his second coming (1 Thess. 4:17; cf. John 14:1–3; 1 Cor. 15:51–52). Some insist that the rapture is only for the church apart from those saved from Adam to Christ. Different facets of this view combine to present the picture of the raptured church in heaven being judged and rewarded and thereafter enjoying a great wedding feast with Christ in the air. It is held also by some that the Holy Spirit will likewise be raptured or taken from the earth at this time. This view also teaches that the rapture will be followed by the great tribulation (Matt. 24:21) or persecution of the Jews by Satan as he endeavors to destroy national Israel. This is also to be a time of divine judgments. The tribulation is to last seven years, after which Christ will return in power and glory. Let us note, however, that Jesus presents the rapture as coming after the tribulation (Matt. 24:29–31). The rapture is certain; the timetable is the question. Does the rapture come before or after the tribulation?

The word "tribulation" both in Hebrew and Greek means distress, pressure, or affliction (Deut. 4:30; Judg. 10:14; 1 Sam. 10:19; 1 Thess. 3:4; Rev. 1:9; 2:9, 22). It is connected with the idea of persecution (Matt. 13:21). In Matthew 24:21 Jesus spoke of suffering connected with the destruction of Jerusalem. To his disciples he said, "In the world ye shall have tribulation" (John 16:33). It is to this latter end that

Jesus refers in Matthew 24:29 ff.: "Immediately after the tribulation of those days shall the sun be darkened." It would seem that tribulation refers not to a post-rapture persecution of the Jews but to the sufferings endured by Christ's followers throughout Christian history (Matt. 24:8–14).

The "beginning of sorrows" in verse 8 suggests not a sign of the end but of the beginning. John A. Broadus said in his *Commentary on Matthew,* "But does not the expression mean that in the preparation for the complete reign of the Messiah, conflict is unavoidable, not simply individual and domestic variance, but conflict of the races and nations, as afterwards depicted in the visions of John on Patmos?" Of interest is the fact that "sorrows" in verse 8 (*thlipsis,* pressure, affliction) is the same word translated in verse 21 (and elsewhere) as the great tribulation. That the tribulation refers to the experience of Christians in proclaiming the gospel is clearly seen in Revelation 1:9; 2:9–10, 22; 7:14. In this light, therefore, it would seem that we can best understand Matthew 24:29–31. The rapture of the saints comes at the end of the tribulation of the saints.

We come now to the question of the millennium. Here we are confronted with one of the greatest of all problems in eschatology. Strange to say, it is based upon one brief passage of Scripture (Rev. 20:1–7). The word "millennium" comes from two Latin words, *mille,* a thousand, and *annus,* year. The Greek words are *chilia,* thousand, and *etos,* year. From the word *chilia* we get the word "chiliasm," which means the same thing as millennium. The millennium, therefore, refers to the thousand-year binding of Satan (Rev. 20:2–3) and Christ's consequent millennial reign (Rev. 20:4). Upon these verses are based several positions in eschatological belief as distinguished by the prefixes post, pre, and a. (For post and pre positions see Mullins, pp. 466 ff.)

Postmillennial refers to those who believe that Christ will return after the thousand-year binding of Satan and that until then the world will become progressively better. By the spread of the gospel, a gradual conquest of evil will be accomplished. At the close of this period, the conflict between good and evil will be renewed for a time, after which Christ will return and there will be the resurrection of all the dead and the final judgment. This is the view held by most liberals or modernists. But strange to say, it was also the position held by many former stalwarts of the faith.

Premillennial denotes the position of those who believe that the world will become progressively worse until Christ returns before the millennium to usher in a thousand years of righteous reign with his saints. During this time Satan will be bound, only to be released for a brief time after the millennium. At his coming Christ will triumph over his enemies and destroy the antichrist (2 Thess. 2:8; Jude 14–15). Living Christians will be caught up to meet the Lord in the air (2 Thess. 4:17) after the resurrection of the dead in Christ (Rev. 20:4–6). Following a preliminary judgment of the living nations, the risen saints will reign with Christ a thousand years (Rev. 20:4; Matt. 25:31–46). Following the thousand years Satan will be loosed for a period of flagrant wickedness (Rev. 20:7–10). After this there will be the resurrection of the wicked, succeeded by the final judgment and eternal rewards (Rev. 20:12–15). It needs to be said, however, that premillennials range all the way from those who hold generally to the above to those who follow elaborately worked out programs as to detailed events. Suffice it to say that neither Jesus nor his inspired writers gave such a detailed and ordered account. It is enough to know that Christ will return; we can leave the details to him.

Amillennial refers to those who hold that the thousand

years are not to be taken literally but are a symbol of a period
of indefinite time. The Greek letter *a* used as a prefix has the
strength of a negative. Amillennium means no millennium.
In support of this view reference is made to 2 Peter 3:8,
where the writer says that with the Lord a thousand years are
as a day and a day as a thousand years. In short, time is irrele-
vant with God. Furthermore, adherents to this view point out
the highly symbolic nature of Revelation. To this group generally the thousand years actually refer to the indefinite period from the earthly ministry of Jesus to the return of the
Lord. During this time Satan is partially bound (Luke 10:18–
19; cf. Mark 3:27). After Satan is loosed, he finds a ready re-
ception (Rev. 20:8–9). Thus they say that the millennium is
the period of struggle between the earthly ministry of Jesus
and his second coming, when Satan's power is limited and
when certain victory is assured to Christ's followers. This last
is referred to as the reigning of Christ's people with him.

II. The Resurrection from the Dead

Having dealt with this in a previous chapter, we shall only
affirm the fact of it and then proceed to the question of a dual
or single resurrection.

1. The dual resurrection theory.—As we have seen, this
theory is a part of the idea of two comings of Christ. According to its adherents, Christ will come secretly for the rapture
of the church. This is regarded as the first resurrection (Rev.
20:5). At the end of the millennium there will be the resurrection of the wicked. Those who hold this view are not clear
as to the resurrection of the Old Testament saints or of
those saved during the millennium.

What is meant by the "first resurrection" in Revelation
20:5 is not too clear. Immediately preceding this verse the
reference is to "martyrs" (Rev. 20:4) who are to reign with

Christ: "But the rest of the dead lived not again until the thousand years were finished" (Rev. 20:5). Do the martyrs refer to all the church or simply to those who died for their faith? Does "rest of the dead" include other saints, apart from the martyrs, along with the wicked? Some amillennialists refer to the first resurrection as the experience of redemption (Eph. 2:1 ff.); all who are in Christ have been raised from the death of trespasses and sins to walk in newness of life (Rom. 6:4), in which we reign with Christ throughout the gospel period (Eph. 2:6–7; cf. Rev. 20:4–6).

However, Paul's word about a first resurrection simply means that "the dead in Christ shall rise first" (1 Thess. 4:16), before living Christians are "caught up together with them in the clouds, to meet the Lord in the air" (1 Thess. 4:17). Elsewhere Paul referred only to the resurrection of the saints without reference to the wicked (1 Cor. 15:50 ff.). Here he was thinking only of saved people. In Acts 24:15, however, he spoke of the resurrection "both of the just and unjust." Jesus spoke of the resurrection of the just (Luke 14:14) but also of the just and the unjust (John 5:29). It would appear that both Jesus and Paul thought of only one resurrection.

2. *The single resurrection theory.*—The New Testament seems to speak of one coming of Christ with one resurrection both of the just and the unjust. The "first resurrection" idea in Revelation 20:5 poses many questions, but in view of the "souls of them that were beheaded for the witness of Jesus" (Rev. 20:4) or martyrs and "the rest of the dead" (Rev. 20:5), plus the fact that there is no specific mention of a second resurrection of the wicked, plus the uses of Jesus and Paul of "the just and the unjust," the evidence shows that one resurrection is taught in the New Testament. This is where our case lies.

III. The Judgment

1. The fact of the judgment.—The principle of judgment runs throughout the Scriptures (Isa. 42:1, 3–4; 61:8; Jer. 4:2; Matt. 10:15; 11:22, 24; 12:36; John 5:22, 27, 30; 16:8; Acts 24:25; Heb. 9:27; 2 Peter 2:4, 9; 3:7; 1 John 4:17; Rev. 14:7).

2. The Judge at the judgment.—The Scriptures plainly teach that Christ will be the judge (Matt. 19:28; 25:31–46; Luke 22:28–30; John 5:22–27; Acts 17:31; Rom. 2:16; Heb. 9:27–28; Rev. 3:21; 20:11 ff.).

3. The subjects of the judgment.—In 2 Corinthians 5:10 Paul said, "For we must all appear before the judgment seat of Christ; that every one may receive the things done in his body, according to that he hath done, whether it be good or bad" (cf. John 5:22–30). The picture of the judgment in Revelation 20:11–15 is most revealing. There the dead, small and great, stand before God. The "books" are opened, and "another book . . . which is the book of life" is also opened. The dead are judged by those things "written in the books, according to their works." "Whosoever was not found written in the book of life was cast into the lake of fire." All men shall be judged. Judgment will be not to determine character but to reveal and declare it. Those whose names are written in the book of life—the redeemed—will be rewarded in heaven according to their works. There will be degrees of reward in heaven and of punishment in hell—according to works (Luke 12:47–48; cf. Matt. 25:13–30; 1 Cor. 3:11–15).

Before passing from this topic we shall do well to consider whether there will be one or many judgments. One school of thought holds to the latter; there will be the judgment of the church immediately following the rapture, and then there will be the judgment of the Jews during the tribulation. Next there will be the judgment of "the living nations" at the beginning of the millennium (Matt. 25:31 ff.). Further, other special judgments will take place during the "rod of iron rule" of Jesus during the millennium. Finally, there will be the "great white throne" judgment (Rev. 20:11–15). However, it would appear that the Scriptures teach one general judgment. Some of these suggested judgments are rather vague. The two distinct descriptions of the judgment certainly are not incompatible with the idea of one judgment (Matt. 25:31 ff.; Rev. 20:11–15). It is difficult to see how Christ could judge nations except in the confines of history. The details of Matthew 25:31 ff. all point to individual judgments, not to corporate ones. The "individual" idea certainly fits the other judgment and also scattered references to it. The preliminary reference to the judgment in Revelation 6:14–17 includes all men, not segments of the human race.

IV. The Nature of the Kingdom

Once more we are dealing with a subject previously treated. The emphasis here will be with regard to the final aspects of Christ's rule. Here again there is a difference of opinion. One school of thought emphasizes the reign of Christ and his saints upon the earth during the millennial period (Rev. 5:10; 20:4; cf. Matt. 19:28; Luke 1:32; Acts 2:30). About the idea of Christ sitting on the throne of David (Luke 1:32; Acts 2:30) is built an elaborate system of thought regarding the restoration of an earthly kingdom patterned after the glorious reign of David and the restoration of the Temple in Jerusalem. It was this emphasis which colored the Jews' conception of the Messiah at the time of the incarnation and which led to their rejection of Jesus. Adherents to the idea of a future earthly reign of Christ insist that this view will be fulfilled at his second coming.

On the other hand, there are those who hold that the Scripture's pointing to such a reign is symbolic of the eternal reign of Christ over all his universe; this began during Jesus' public ministry and will culminate in heaven. They insist that David's reign, as the most glorious of the earthly Israel, is symbolic of this greater reign of the Christ. Without entering into this problem let us simply state that the message of Revelation is the final and complete victory of Christ over all his enemies and his resultant reign over all his universe (Rev. 3:21; 4; 7:10 ff.; 22:1, 3) . Paul clearly states the matter. After the resurrection, "then cometh the end, when he shall have delivered up the kingdom to God, even the Father; when he shall have put down all rule and all authority and power. For he must reign, till he hath put all enemies under his feet. The last enemy that shall be destroyed is death. . . . And when all things [the universe] shall be subdued unto him, then shall the Son also himself be subject unto him that put all things under him, that God may be all in all" (1 Cor. 15:24–28) .

When Jesus ascended after the resurrection, he sat down "on the right hand of the throne of the Majesty in the heavens" (Heb. 8:1; cf. 12:2) , "from henceforth expecting till his enemies be made his footstool" (Heb. 10:12–13; cf. Phil. 2:5–11) . It would seem that his reign from heaven began at that time and will continue until all his enemies shall be subdued (Rev. 20) , after which the Son will deliver the kingdom to the Father, and God and the Lamb (Rev. 22:3) shall reign forever. The redeemed will participate in that reign as the willing servants of God (Rev. 22:3–5) . The prospect is glorious! The details we leave with him.

To conclude this study let us summarize the doctrine of last things. At the end, a time known only to God, "the Lord himself shall descend from heaven with a shout, with the voice of the archangel, and with the trump of God" (1 Thess. 4:16; 1 Cor. 15:52). Suddenly he will come "as a thief in the night; in the which the heavens shall pass away with a great noise, and the elements shall melt with fervent heat, the earth also and the works that are therein shall be burned up. . . . Nevertheless we [the saved], according to his promise, look for new heavens and a new earth, wherein dwelleth righteousness" (2 Peter 3:10 ff.; cf. Rev. 21:1). It will be a time of great terror for the unsaved, who will hide "themselves in the dens and in the rocks of the mountains; and said to the mountains and rocks, Fall on us, and hide us from the face of him that sitteth on the throne, and from the wrath of the Lamb" (Rev. 6:15–16). But it will be a time of rejoicing for the redeemed (2 Tim. 4:8), for "the dead in Christ shall rise first: then we which are alive and remain shall be caught up together with them in the clouds, to meet the Lord in the air: and so shall we ever be with the Lord" (1 Thess. 4:16–17). At the same time the unsaved dead will be raised (John 5:28–29) to join in terror the unsaved who are alive at Christ's coming (Rev. 1:7; 6:15–16; 20:11).

Then all men shall appear for judgment before the great white throne (Rev. 20:11–15). The saved will be glorified and rewarded according to their works and will enter into the indescribable bliss of eternal heaven (Rev. 21–22). The lost shall be doomed and punished according to their works in the indescribable anguish of eternal hell (Rev. 20:15).